MILLER'S

BUYING
AFFORDABLE
ART

MILLER'S

BUYING
AFFORDABLE
ART

HUGH ST. CLAIR

BUYING AFFORDABLE ART
By Hugh St. Clair

First published in Great Britain in 2005
by Miller's, a division of Mitchell Beazley,
imprints of Octopus Publishing Group Ltd,
2–4 Heron Quays, London E14 4JP

Miller's is a registered trademark of Octopus Publishing Ltd

While every care has been taken in the compilation of this book,
neither the publishers nor the author can accept any liability for any
financial or other loss incurred by reliance placed on the information
contained in this book

Prices are given in the currency of the country where the sale took place.
Most prices are given their equivalent in US dollars or pounds sterling at
a rate of $1.8 to £1. Past prices have equivalents worked out at their
appropriate contemporary exchange rate.

ISBN 1 84533 041 2

A CIP record for this book is available from the British Library

Set in Frutiger and Eurostile

Printed and bound in the UK by Mackays of Chatham, Ltd

Senior Executive Editor Anna Sanderson
Executive Art Editor Rhonda Summerbell
Editor Catherine Emslie
Copy Editor Claire Musters
Production Jane Rogers
Proofreader Barbara Mellor
Indexer Sue Farr

CONTENTS

FOREWORD

Buying a work of art is not easy. To buy something worthwhile you will probably have to spend in excess of £500 ($900), so you don't want to get it wrong. Buying art is not like buying a car or a pair of curtains; you have to lead rather than follow. For example, your neighbour may recommend their Volkswagen, so you decide to buy one exactly the same. However you can't buy the same painting as your neighbour's, or order one from an interior design magazine – the decision is entirely yours. If you are spending £1,000 ($1,800) on a painting you are not going to hide it away. This work of art is going to be prominently displayed for all to see, and all, potentially, to judge.

I have written this book to take the anxiety out of buying works of art. My aim is to guide you through an important purchase that will be far more exciting than buying a car or a sofa. It is a purchase that can give you pleasure for the rest of your life – and possibly the lives of your descendants too.

These days, when buying art the choice is greater than ever before, with new art fairs opening all over Europe and the United States. In England alone there are said to be more working artists today than there were in the entire Italian Renaissance, which lasted for over a century.

As I have already mentioned, you are unlikely to find a good contemporary artist selling their work for much less than £500 ($900) – artists have to eat and pay rent too! Also, in an age of mass communication, when it is easier to research art and artists, people are more aware of prices and therefore unwilling to let good paintings go for nothing. However, you don't always need a vast disposable income to form an excellent personal art collection. Indeed, some of the best collections have been formed by enthusiasts of very modest means (*see* p.143–4).

This book will give you all the confidence and inspiration you need to start your very own collection of affordable art. It reveals how you can make informed purchases, and how to choose an artist whose work could well keep its value – or even be worth more in years to come. Unlike a car, a good painting should not substantially decrease in value after leaving the saleroom.

Information is given on all the visual arts – paintings and drawings, prints, photography, posters, and sculpture – as well as a commentary on the new multimedia artwork age. Each section includes a concise history with explanations of art terms and methods. This is particularly important in the field of photographs and posters, where there is a surprising number of wily sellers passing off laser-printed items as the genuine thing.

Details of who and what commands the highest prices, and where affordable investments can be made, are also provided, and a multitude of questions answered: where are the best places to buy and sell art, how can you find out whether that filthy oil painting you found in a junk shop is worth anything, what are the tax implications if you inherit a work of art or if you want to pass it on to your children? And once you have finally made your all-important purchase, there is advice on how to display, light, care for, and possibly restore your newest prized possession.

In addition to the Useful Contacts & Reference provided at the end of each chapter, at the end of the book a directory supplies details of further auction houses, museums, and galleries, in addition to a bibliography, and a list of periodicals – all intended to offer a valuable springboard to learning more about appreciating and buying art.

INTRODUCTION TO BUYING ART

"Pleasure is the root of all critical appreciation of art."
Robert Hughes

What you will learn in this chapter:

- The reasons why people buy art
- Whether it is worth investing in art in today's market
- What affects the price of art
- Where the centre of the art world is

We all know that feeling – the thrill, the "tingling spine" – when we see something beautiful that would bring us immeasurable pleasure and happiness if we owned it. For some people it's a new kitchen, for others a pair of beautiful black suede boots. For me, and many others, it's a painting, a sculpture, or a drawing. The most important reason for buying a work of art is because it brings pleasure and satisfaction.

Works of art are not bought just for financial reasons. Personal satisfaction is a priceless benefit. Buying a picture because it says something to you personally is the most important criterion to consider – not "when can I sell it on?" We may all sneer at large corporations which buy very expensive paintings only to keep them in a safe, but it would be equally depressing to have a work of art on your wall that you didn't like but had been persuaded to buy as a worthwhile investment. You would probably spend your life worrying all the time about when and how to sell it, but selling a painting is not as easy as disposing of a stock or bond.

Works of art are not part of life's essentials in the way that food, clothes, and a place to live are. Many people see buying art as a bit of an indulgence, and can feel guilty that they are not paying off some of the mortgage or putting the money into a savings account for a rainy day. Consequently they tend to justify their purchases by saying that pictures are a good investment and will always increase in value.

The volume of practising artists has increased dramatically over the centuries, so how do you separate the wheat from the chaff? A huge proportion of works created today will not appreciate in value; indeed they might even decrease.

ART VERSUS STOCKS & SHARES

Art is no longer tied to the stock market. It is viewed as an inflation hedge. Why keep your money in a falling stock market or in a bank or building society that pays very little interest, when you could buy a picture? Also, in times of high monetary inflation it makes good sense to put money into something tangible, such as a work of art.

Art is an excellent way of saving spare cash, too. If you buy a work of art with a company bonus, after a few years you'll be glad that you spent the money on something that has probably appreciated in value (if you made a wise choice) rather than on clothes or a car, for example. How often have you heard people cry, "I had all that money and now I've got nothing to show for it"?

Art is a good long-term investment. True, it doesn't pay an income until you sell it – unlike stocks and shares, which pay regular dividends providing you have a decent stockbroker. However, you should get a decent capital sum in the end, when you really need it. (Please note, I have purposely used the word "should" here because, both in stocks and shares and in art investment, there are no certainties. I will attempt to show that there are certain steps you can take to minimize risk when investing in a work of art, but it is impossible to predict the future, and random occurrences can affect prices – *see* "What Affects the Price of Art", p.13).

A piece of art is something beautiful that you can admire every day; a share certificate can't give that kind of pleasure. However, works of art have to be insured and kept clean and in good condition in order to maintain their value. Stocks and shares do not incur this extra cost.

You can sell a stock quickly if you need to, but getting the best price for your work of art might take some time. To achieve maximum value, the work needs to be put into the most suitable auction and these might occur only every few months. Once it is sold you could also wait for up to 30 days to actually receive your money. If you use an art dealer they have to find the right buyer, and this can take time. If a buyer is not immediately forthcoming, and you want to get rid of something quickly, a dealer is likely to buy at a lower, trade price. He or she will take into consideration money tied up in stock (your artwork) and will then sell it at a higher retail price. Dealers are in business to make money, and they also have to store your artwork.

Putting something back into auction too soon after you have bought it is also inadvisable. Dealers, who make up a large proportion of buyers at auction, would see the work as shop-soiled. They will start to ask questions: why is it being returned for sale so quickly? Is there something wrong with it? Has the buyer found that the auction house has misattributed the picture and it is worth much less than he/she paid for it?

Perhaps surprisingly, if you had invested a substantial sum in the stock market in 1970, rather than in either houses or paintings, you would have made more money. There are, of course exceptions to this. No company is a totally safe bet: many large and supposedly safe businesses have gone out of business in the past 35 years. Also, some pictures and sculptures, mostly at the top end of the art market, have risen stratospherically in value more than house prices and many stocks. For example, if you had bought one of the young British artist Damien Hirst's early pieces and sold it again in 2004 you would have made an absolute killing. Rare, very fine pieces and work by fashionable artists who are in the public eye tend to increase in value far more than good but rather ordinary works.

Given all the above, I suppose my advice would be that if you love dealing and studying the financial pages of the newspapers then you should deal in stocks and shares, and if you love decorating houses and are prepared to move every few years, invest in property. Art enthusiasts should buy art in order to own something that they love and that could provide a nest egg in the future. This is in some ways the best of all worlds.

HOW THE ART MARKET HAS PERFORMED

The art market, like stocks and shares but unlike property prices, was affected by the invasion of Iraq and acts of terrorism. Following 9/11, people who might have gone to London, Paris, or New York to see an art exhibition or to attend an auction were more cautious about flying and buying. Following the invasion of Iraq people did start to travel again, but they were still worried about the outcome of the war and how it might affect the world economy.

The *Art Sales Index* publishes its extensive findings about the trade in art annually. It found that after 9/11 there was a steady decline in the number of pictures sold for over £1 million. In 2001 before 9/11, 215 works were sold totalling £658 million ($985 million). In 2002 the figure dropped to 186, which fetched £522 million ($760 million), and in 2003 just 149 works sold for £363 million ($580 million). Later, the international art market shrank by 10 per cent from £1.63 billion in the 12-month period to August 2003. Great Britain saw the greatest decline in its turnover, with an 18 per cent fall, while the United States saw an overall fall of 11 per cent.

However, the downturn in the art market did finally begin to change in 2004. The highest price paid for a picture in 2002–3 was £17.6 million ($27 million) for a Renaissance picture, Mantegna's *Descent into Limbo*, which was bought by an anonymous collector. Nobody, therefore, could ever have predicted the mind-boggling sum of $104 million (£58 million) that Picasso's *Boy with a Pipe* fetched in 2004. This became the highest price ever paid for a single picture, overtaking Van Gogh's *Portrait of Dr Gachet*, which had sold for $74 million (£46 million) in New York 14 years earlier. The Picasso had belonged to one of America's "first families", the Whitneys, and was originally estimated at $70 million (£40 million). John Whitney, a former United States ambassador to Great Britain, had bought the picture for $30,000 (£10,700) in 1950, and so made a tidy profit.

It is certainly true that there was increased expenditure on art in 2004. Spending on art in Britain in 2004 was £3 billion ($5.4 billion), up threefold in just two years. According to the *Art Price Index* there was also a renewed air of confidence among American buyers in 2004. Turnover at fine-art auctions jumped by more than 30 per cent on the previous year and there was an increase in the good-quality work that was available, particularly at the top end of the market. The *Art Price Index* also noted that there was a noticeable increase in the contemporary art segment in the United States, and in Europe too, as they recorded that receipts for contemporary art sales had doubled over the previous year.

WHAT IS THE RIGHT PRICE FOR A WORK OF ART?

The famous art critic Robert Hughes, author of *The Shock of the New*, thundered that the exorbitant price paid for Picasso's *Boy with a Pipe* was a "cultural obscenity". He maintained that something is very rotten in the world. Even Picasso's biographer John Richardson observed that no painting should be worth that much.

But who can say what is too much, or too little? In the 1890s a Scottish illustrator named A.J. Hartrick (an acquaintance of Vincent Van Gogh) had noticed Van Gogh's *Still Life with Apples* for sale in a Paris gallery for 10 francs (£1). He liked the picture a lot, but decided 10 francs was a high price to pay at the time for a relatively unknown artist. He didn't buy the painting and spent a lifetime regretting that decision. The point is that the price for this piece was considered too high at the time, and the picture remained in the gallery window, unsold, for months.

So what is too high or too low a price to pay? Why did the buyer pay so far over the estimate for Picasso's *Boy with a Pipe*? What troubles so many people (including critics) is that, in their opinion, better works of art than *Boy with a Pipe* sell for less money. But price does not necessarily reflect quality. Buying a Picasso or a Van Gogh has almost become a competition for the super rich.

So, on a more affordable level, how do you know that the price is right? The answer is that you don't. Dr Hartrick probably should have bought the picture. He might have thought the price high, but he liked it and he could afford it. That should be the main criterion for buying an unknown at auction today, too. If you like it, decide your upper limit and be prepared to go up to it.

WHAT AFFECTS THE PRICE OF ART?

There are many factors involved, but here is an overview:

The economy When the economy is strong more people have more money to spend on art. Auction prices rise as a result, owing to a larger pool of competing bidders. In particular, when a country becomes economically successful, prices for home-grown art tend to rise, partly because economic growth seems to generate nationalist sentiments, which may be expressed in the buying of works of art. However, in a similar way to property prices, art continues to rise in price long after the economy has slowed down. People move money out of the stock market into houses or pictures. After a long period of growth the stock market fell back at the turn of the 21st century, but artworks were still fetching good prices. Then the unexpected catastrophe of 9/11 happened and Americans stopped travelling to England. But in France the auction houses were denationalized at the end of 2001, allowing Sotheby's and Christie's to operate more freely there, with increased prosperity.

Fashion Even in the art world, fashions change over the years and certain styles and artists may become more sought after than they used to be. This obviously pushes the price up.

Style and reputation The price of artists' work usually increases as their style matures. Dealers often take on a young artist straight from college and increase the cost of his or her work over time, based on the success of the last show and the publicity it gained. If an artist's first show is a sell-out, with a waiting list for new pictures, then higher prices will be charged in the future.

"The auction room, as anyone knows, is an excellent medium for sustaining fictional price levels, because the public imagines that auction prices are necessarily real prices." Robert Hughes

Publicity Art will also rise in value if there has recently been an exhibition devoted to an artist or art movement at a major city art gallery, or there has been a book or television programme about an artist. The publicity and exposure will attract investors' attention, and the buying public might come to appreciate works of art they did not previously know about.

Size and material New artists often price their work according to size and material. Go to a show by a new artist and you will find that large oils in ornate frames will cost more than a tiny pencil sketch. An artist at his or her first exhibition often has no other way of charging except by how long it took them to execute the work and how much the materials cost.

Equally, when an artist has gained a reputation, the value of individual pieces depends on the medium. For example, a small sketch or pencil landscape by Gainsborough will fetch less than a full-length portrait in oil. At a more affordable level, if a painting costs £1,000 ($1,800), you could probably pick up a drawing by the same artist for half the price or less. Over recent centuries, auction houses and the art establishment have decided what artists do best. Gainsborough is well known for his portraits of society ladies, but he also painted less well-known, and consequently cheaper, landscapes.

DO RECORD PRICES AFFECT AFFORDABLE ART?

The gigantic price paid for the *Boy with a Pipe* does not mean that the price of all other Picasso oils will rise in proportion to this. The *Boy with a Pipe* is considered to be one of Picasso's masterpieces. A friend of Picasso, André Salmon, recalled the conception of the painting. Apparently the picture was originally intended to show an ordinary Parisian workman, but Salmon wrote that one evening Picasso left his friends to return to the studio and work on this canvas, which he had not touched for a month. He painted a crown of roses on the boy, and critics believe that this was what transformed the picture into a masterpiece. The crown of roses elevated the boy from being a mere workman to a figure of androgynous significance. In this single decision Picasso broke with the 19th-century convention that men should be painted engaged in virile pursuits or propping up swooning women.

However, the high prices attained by certain artists and schools do impact on other areas of art: as Impressionism and Modern art become prohibitively expensive, for example, so art investors switch to more affordable and available pictures, in turn causing these to rise in value.

High-profile figures buying particular works may also produce surges of interest. For example Guy Ritchie, husband of the pop star Madonna, is reputedly keen to buy some Old Masters. If this is indeed the case the publicity will attract other buyers and investors to that field. Drawings in the genre, which are relatively inexpensive, will also rise in value.

WHAT DETERMINES THE PRICE OF INDIVIDUAL PIECES?

Buying and selling raises the price of art A prolific artist produces more work, so there is more to buy and sell than with an artist who produces few works. To illustrate this let us look at Pop art contemporaries Mel Ramos and Andy Warhol. Ramos did not paint a great number of pictures; Warhol, on the other hand, left many pictures and signed prints. There are not enough Ramos works on the market for speculators. Artists need to be kept in the public eye, and that happens through their work changing hands frequently.

More people know about Warhol than about Ramos. Warhol has a graduated price list, with the best changing hands for huge sums but lesser works being much cheaper. Dealers know that for high-quality works of art they can ask as much as they think a client will pay. For example, if a dealer has a piece that has never been on the market before, from a not very prolific but highly regarded artist, it will certainly do well, but in the future prices will not rise as much as they would for an artist who has produced a huge volume of work.

Auctions and dealers can raise prices The value of established artists selling at auction may be over-inflated by competing collectors who are keen to outbid each other in an effort to purchase a piece. In a saleroom it is therefore essentially just a few people who bid up the prices, but an unexpectedly high hammer price, for whatever reason, will still set the new benchmark for the work. Dealers will buy good work at bargain prices, raising the price of an artist by buying up as much of his or her work as they can and making examples scarce. They then release the work slowly and at considerably increased prices.

With more art fairs more business is being done The Affordable Art Fair started in London in 1999 with the aim of selling art for under £5,000 ($9,000). Now, in addition to two in London, there are Affordable Art Fairs in Bristol, New York, Sydney, and Melbourne. In 1999 the turnover at the British fairs totalled £1 million ($1.6 million), five years later their turnover was over £6 million ($11 million), and it continues to increase. People are certainly buying more pictures. The *Frieze* Art Fair opened in London in 2003 and is now an important fixture in the calendar of contemporary art collectors. In 2001 a new art show, Art Basel Miami Beach, a similar event to the long-established and famous Art Basel in Switzerland, was also started.

Art is now being marketed more glamorously Before it spawned an art fair, *Frieze* was a glossy magazine founded at the beginning of the 21st century to appeal to 21st-century tastes. With its flashy cover lines and smart layout it feels more like a fashion magazine than a dry, academic publication. At the same time the London-based *Art Review* was revamped into a glossy magazine that describes itself on the cover as "*Art Review*, international art and style". Art is increasingly being marketed in the same way as clothes and cars for style-conscious professionals with disposable incomes. New art magazines today are unlikely to use the words "Journal" or "Quarterly" in their titles. The new readers that are being sought by these magazines are all potential art investors. *Flash Art*, which calls itself the "World's leading art magazine", was founded in Italy in the early 1980s and is another excellent example of the new, glamorous approach to marketing art.

Artists as celebrities Andy Warhol is the most obvious example of the celebrity cult of the artist. With the growth of more diverse media and a greater number of magazines and television shows, editors and producers are willing to focus on artists just as they do on Hollywood film stars. Celebrity status, or in some cases notoriety, sells and creates a demand, causing the artist's work to rise in price.

The death of an artist Although extremely sad, the early death of an artist can cause their work to become collectable and, with a finite number of pieces available, prices to rise. Since the death of Sarah Raphael at the young age of 41 in 2004, the prices of this much-lauded artist have been rising steadily. In some cases, however, artists are completely neglected immediately after their death. Henri Gaudier-Brzeska was a handsome and romantic figure who was killed in his 20s in the First World War. After his death his work was largely ignored until it was rescued by Jim Ede (*see* "Notable Collectors", pp.143–4). During the 20th century Gaudier-Brzeska became the subject of a book and film and prices for his work continue to rise. For example, a sculpture entitled *Maternity* was given an estimate of £12,000 ($21,500) by Sotheby's in 2004, but actually sold for £49,200 ($88,560).

AUCTION RECORDS

Asking prices are determined by recent auction records, as these are the best way of gauging current market interest in a particular artist or type of work. There are a number of organizations that collate auction records, as well as artists' biographies (*see* "Useful Contacts & Reference", p.20). Their fees vary: some require large annual subscriptions while others will allow you to pay per view.

The *Art Sales Index*, for example, is available via the Internet and has over 2.8 million entries on fine art by 215,000 artists. Another, Artprice.com, claims to be the world leader in art market information and reports trends in the market. It can be viewed in English, French, Spanish, and German and has a databank of 21 million auction prices and 306,000 artists in a variety of media from auction houses worldwide. You can check if the signature on your piece is correct by comparing it to their extensive database of artists' monograms, symbols, and signatures.

Such price indices can be taken only as a guideline, not as an immutable certainty. The value of works of art by one artist can vary wildly depending on condition and when the work was executed.

WHAT MAKES PRICES FALL?

Any art expert will recall the crash of Impressionist art in the late 1980s, when values fell by half. There were two reasons for this. Firstly, people thought that Impressionist art, whatever its quality, would just keep on going up and up, and stupid prices were being paid by speculators. The result was that the market in Impressionist art became overheated. Secondly, many of the speculators were Japanese, and around this time the Japanese economy went into a serious downturn. It took around ten years for prices of Impressionist works and some American Modern art to recover and reach mid-1980s prices again. The lesson to draw from this is that you should buy with discernment, rather than buying anything by a particular artist. Artists have off days just like everyone else.

WHERE IS THE CENTRE OF THE ART WORLD?

France, of course, was where artists flocked to in the middle of the 20th century. An artist's credibility was much enhanced if he or she studied in Paris or lived in an artists' colony in the south of France. However, London and New York are where art is sold today. For some time now London has been the centre of the art world. British firms Sotheby's and Christie's are the market leaders, with offices around the world. London has had an advantage over continental Europe because buyers, art dealers, and collectors have not had to pay a resale royalty known as the *droit de suite*, which is currently in force in some European countries and applicable to all members of the EU from 2006.

In recent years rents have risen enormously in areas of London and New York. As a result, art galleries selling affordable art in downtown Manhattan, for example, have found it harder to make enough money. Some have therefore moved to cheaper Brooklyn. Although still very important, New York no longer has the monopoly on good art galleries in the United States. New and interesting galleries are opening in Chicago and Los Angeles, which both have a thriving art scene. One Angeleno artist, Phil Bower, used to be of the opinion that you had to show in New York to be considered a serious artist. Now, with a new art complex opening in a former railway station in Santa Monica, the Bergamot Station, and numerous very trendy galleries in Culver City, he is quite happy to live and work in California. A similar shift is happening in London, where some of the city's hippest and newest galleries have moved out of the expensive West End to the cheaper East End.

London and New York will always be two of the most important "art cities", but other cities, especially Chicago and Miami, are also becoming important centres for art fairs, and are where an increasing band of local collectors buy their art. Art fairs, just like any other business, are attracted to an area by favourable venue rents, good and inexpensive local hotels and restaurants, and, most importantly, a concentration of new, affluent collectors who might not make special trips to London and New York, but are keen to spend their money on art.

Local supply also determines where auctions are held. Pictures of major international importance are not likely to be sold in Miami, Los Angeles, or a provincial British city, but rather in New York or London, and sometimes Switzerland (if, for example, a rich resident is selling his or her collection of Impressionist pictures and there are tax advantages for the vendor). However, it stands to reason that you are more likely to find a selection of affordable 18th-century pictures and Scottish landscapes in British auction houses, such as those in Bath and Edinburgh, and mid-20th century abstract paintings in American auction houses in Cincinnati and St Louis.

USEFUL CONTACTS & REFERENCE
AUCTION RECORDS
Artfact.com To check prices visit this website, which lists the sale value of over 5 million works of art sold since 1986. Search by keyword, price range, and artist.

Artnet.com This website presents auction results from over 500 international auction houses since 1985.

Artprice.com You can search this database, written in French and English, by artist or work for future sale. It also lists past sales records and provides an analysis of the state of the art market. As well as being available over the Internet, it produces books and CD-ROMs that are specific to the fine art and photography markets. For specific art investment, email artinvestment@artprice.com or call +33 (0)472 421 707.

(Hislop's) Art Sales Index Found on the shelves of most major public libraries, this annual prints prices reached for European (including British), North American (including Canada), Australian, and New Zealand artists. It has over 2.8 million entries of fine art by 215,000 artists. Visit www.art-sales-index.com or call +44 (0)1784 451 145 to order the book.

Gordons USA-based, Gordons specialize in print and photography records. They too are available over the Internet for a fee and also produce books. Visit their website www.gordonsart.com, or call them on +1 602 253 6948.

FAIRS, MAGAZINES, & SHOWS
See p.189 for more periodicals.

Art Basel Held in Basel, Switzerland in June and featuring work by some 2,000 artists. The Miami Beach version is in December. Visit www.artbasel.com for further information.

Art Review This magazine covers up-and-coming artists and trends and includes a calendar of shows for the month. Available in the US and UK: for more information call +44 1858 438803 or visit www.art-review.com.

Flash Art This magazine sees itself as international; there's nothing in great depth but it's a romp through what is happening, from Bejing to Baltimore. Published by Giancarlo Politi Editore, Italy. Visit www.flashartonline.com or call +39 02 6887341.

Frieze **Art Fair** Every October, this London art fair is the most exciting and cutting-edge in the city. Visit www.friezeartfair.com or call +44 207 025 3970. For an insight into London's contemporary art world *Frieze* is the magazine to buy – visit www.frieze.com or call +44 (0)1795 414977.

WHAT IS ART?

"Great art is supposed to reflect the truth."
anon

What you will learn in this chapter:
- How art has changed over the centuries
- How fashion can influence people's perception of art
- What art should be and what is "good art"
- How you can learn more about art

Once upon a time in Europe, art was something executed by an artist trained at an academy; the production of a recognizable, realistic image. A castle was a castle and a person a person – even if they were set in mythical landscapes. By the late 19th century the Impressionists had changed all of this. They argued that a painting need not necessarily be an exact representation: it could also be an impression, or a hazy approximation. From then on art became more and more abstract and distant from traditional painting. Yves Klein, for example, simply covered his canvas with blue paint, and the now perhaps infamous artist Tracey Emin even exhibited her unmade bed. The stranglehold of the academies of Europe, who for centuries had told the public what constituted art, was broken in the 20th century.

THE CHANGING FACE OF ART

Because art no longer needs to be purely an exact reproduction, some people nowadays are prepared to pay millions for a canvas painted in different shades of red, while others simply do not understand the point of it. Instead of depicting classical scenes or scenes from legend, artists have turned their attention elsewhere. For example, in 20th-century America some artists, such as Andy Warhol, depicted the new religion – consumerism. Warhol made Marilyn Monroe and Campbell's soup tins his icons, rather than the Virgin Mary or bowls of fruit.

In the past oriental art was strictly stylized, with artists following certain conventions and rules. However, in the 20th century, with the rise of mass communication, oriental artists have absorbed ideas from other parts of the world. China now has modern artists working in a variety of styles (see p.103, "Affordable Fields To Consider Now").

Art from Africa and Australia has always been more naïve, although the techniques and styles for making religious icons and pottery were passed down from generation to generation. There was no formal academy system in either of these continents. Western artists have taken much from Africa – for example, Picasso was fascinated by African artefacts.

The argument still rages on about what constitutes art. How often have you heard a comment such as "My five-year-old grandson could have painted that!" in response to an abstract slosh of paint on a canvas?

Today, the art establishment accepts the notion that art can be an idea, a comment on today's world, and not necessarily a rendition of a religious scene, a recognizable landscape, or a portrait on canvas.

Art critics and commentators consider resistance to certain art to be rooted, in part, in the dual feeling that the spectator has to work too hard, or that the artist didn't work hard enough or long enough to create the piece. Even today, some of us have difficulty in understanding why a naïvely drawn bunch of flowers should be worth more than a meticulously executed landscape. The flowers may be sketchy, but maybe they have an atmospheric quality the landscape lacks. Meticulous accuracy is no longer a criterion for judging a picture.

THE NOTION OF ART NEEDS TO BE CONSTANTLY RE-EVALUATED

In a recent British newspaper survey, readers voted Marcel Duchamp and his famous men's urinal, signed "R. Mutt", the most influential artwork of the 20th century. *Fountain*, as it was called, changed our view on what is art and has been credited with founding Modern art.

However, not everyone took to Carl Andre's *Equivalent VIII* (1966), which was bought by the Tate Gallery in London. British newspapers huffed and puffed for weeks and people who didn't normally discuss art began to do so. "I know better than the people at the Tate Gallery who bought a pile of bricks and called it art. I call it a pile of bricks and that's what it is", wrote Bernard Levin in *The Times*. The Tate called the work informal minimalism. Art writer John Asbury takes a different view from Levin: "What matters is the artist's will to discover, rather than the manual skills he may share with hundreds of other artists. Anybody could have discovered America but only Columbus did", he argues. Carl Andre himself wrote, "I like art works which sort of ambush you, that in a sense take you by surprise. I don't like art that dominates you and is assailing you. I like work that is just there until it needs you and you need it."

THE EFFECT OF FASHION & TRENDS

What is seen as a great work of art is often dictated by fashion, and not always by the competence and beauty of the work. In Rembrandt's time, a flower painter called Van Huysum could command more money than Rembrandt. However, in 2003 a Van Huysum sold for a record price, but it was well below the amount paid for a Rembrandt. And although at the moment paintings by 20th-century artists such as Gauguin and Picasso are worth more than the Old Masters, in the future that might also change. Equally, Californian Impressionism was considered a poor relation of European Impressionism, but it is now increasing in value. Here are some other pointers to bear in mind about trends:

People react against the last generation's taste Prices for paintings go up and down because one generation reacts against another. However, the new generation is usually interested in what their grandparents liked. This is because many people are nostalgic for a style that was popular just before they were born.

A good example of this was the rise in price of Victorian pictures in the 1970s–80s. The generation who were buying art in the 1930s could just remember their parents' Victorian taste, and wanted to buy something different, whereas their children couldn't and had the excitement of discovering very competent Victorian pictures at low prices. Composer Andrew Lloyd Webber was one of those people, and he now has one of the best collections of Victorian pictures in the whole of Britain.

Today, mid-20th-century European and American work is being looked into by a generation who were born just after the artists were at their peak. Similarly, only a few years ago, good-quality modern British art (work produced in 1950–2000) could be picked up for very little, but not anymore.

Fashions change Today, around the world, great consternation surrounds Conceptual art (see p.175) and crazy prices are being paid for pieces. Of course the major players will always be sought after, especially if they are in museum collections, but imitators and followers could well drop in price as the years pass. During the 1960s, Pop art was hyped in Britain in the same way as the young British artists of the 1990s, such as Damien Hirst, but prices fell over time. Watch out, however, as they could rise in value again if the next generation of art collectors becomes interested.

The question is, in reaction to 20th-century Modernism will traditional styles – for example, fine still-lifes in the manner of Dutch 17th-century masters, but painted in 1995 – become collectable? It is impossible to predict, but interesting to watch. Currently, most buyers want Modern art, not 18th-century landscapes or Old Masters. Inherited Victorian or Georgian furniture is now deemed unfashionable, and quirky, ethnic, or modern furniture in plastic or leather creates a look that does not match a pretty 19th-century watercolour.

> **BUYERS' TIP**
> Avoid buying at the top of the market when things are fashionable:
> you will never make any money that way.

The influence of collectors and dealers Fashion can be
changed by influential collectors and dealers who, by buying a
painting or sculpture, can make an artist's reputation. The most
famous of these is Londoner Charles Saatchi, whose purchase
of works by Damien Hirst, Tracey Emin, and many others of that
generation enhanced their reputation and value. When Saatchi
buys, the art world watches carefully, and nowadays his new
favourites are reported in the press. When Saatchi buys an artist
their value rises automatically, such is his power. And one dealer
is of the opinion that the reason that work by a good artist he
knows can still be bought cheaply is that this artist refuses to
sell to Saatchi.

   In January 2005 Saatchi showed paintings in traditional
oils. A statement from his gallery reads, "painting continues
to be the most relevant and vital way that artists choose to
communicate". So he who was once very influential in making
traditional painting unfashionable is now championing it.

READ ART CRITICISM CAREFULLY

As art appreciation is so personal, be aware that art critics are just as
susceptible to personal preference as you are. Of course they have
seen more than you or I, that is their job, so they can make informed
criticism, but they would be inhuman if they didn't judge subjectively.
So if you really like a piece, don't be put off if a critic doesn't.

   There is, for example, the well-known story of Victorian art critic
John Ruskin. In 1875, when reviewing *Nocturne in Black and Gold:
the Falling Rocket* by James Abbott McNeill Whistler, Ruskin wrote,
"I have seen and heard much of cockney impudence before now,
but never expected to hear a coxcomb ask two hundred guineas for
flinging a pot of paint in the public's face." Whistler sued, and

opened up an important debate about the nature of art. Although he won only a farthing (¼p) in damages, he paved the way for Modern art. The most interesting exchange in the trial came when Ruskin's defence asked, "The labour of two days, is that for which you ask two hundred guineas?" and Whistler responded, "No, I ask it for the knowledge I have gained in the work of a lifetime".

BUYERS' TIP

The secret of canny buying is to look out for well-executed pieces by an artist who was once well thought of, but who has become unfashionable and inexpensive. Quality always shines through, irrespective of trends, so such bargains are a good investment.

The shock of the new will wear off This is illustrated well by the story of the Impressionists and other artists working at the turn of the 19th and 20th centuries. They were forced to put on their own shows, and some of today's most sought-after artists, such as Toulouse-Lautrec, sold their work in exchange for food or drink because no one would buy it. Even as late as the 1920s, a critic for *Connoisseur* magazine, on seeing French Modern art by that time in the hands of passionate collectors, remarked in his review, "The half dozen works by Cézanne make one wonder how this painter's great reputation has been achieved, since he neither attempted realism nor did he succeed in attaining a decorative effect". Of Seurat, whose work now has pride of place in all the major museums of the world, the same critic observed, "Seurat's landscape is an effort realistically to express the effect of a broad expanse of herbage seen under ordinary atmospheric conditions, but the result is an impression completely lacking in pictorial interest."

The climate has changed dramatically in recent years, and many more people are receptive to contemporary art. We are less shocked than people used to be by new innovations, more wryly amused. Tracey Emin's famous *Unmade Bed* bemused many people, but there were no calls for her to be drummed out of town for being a fraud. Indeed, nowadays the quirkier a piece is, the more visitors it can draw. The Tate Modern in London and the Guggenheim in New York show avant garde work and pull in crowds from all over the world – people who 15 years ago would never have countenanced a visit to see such things.

BLUE-CHIP ART

In an age of designer labels, the signature on a painting is becoming more and more vital. "Blue chip" refers to artists who have an international name and have had solo exhibitions in museums and galleries worldwide. Blue chip is originally a city term, referring to a large and prestigious company of the highest class: a safe investment because it is unlikely to go bankrupt. This American expression derives from the game of poker in which blue chips are the highest valued in the game. Blue-chip artists include the 20th-century Impressionists, Picasso, and American mid-20th-century artists such as Andy Warhol and Jackson Pollock. Blue-chip art is expensive, but if you can afford it its values do not really decline. These works are safe investments that will not gain or lose huge amounts. A sketch, drawing, or even print by a blue-chip artist is a good place to start. Whether the artist has painted finely detailed oils or, in the case of Matisse, a simple paper collage, the work is blue chip. Unfortunately, the same paper collage done by you or me would merely be a craft piece. What is art and what is craft has been an argument raging for years. The value of Matisse's collage would be taken within his whole canon of work. The work sells because it is by him.

An increasing number of living artists are becoming blue chip, such as painter Damien Hirst and sculptor Anish Kapoor. Investing and buying contemporary blue-chip art is very difficult, because by the time an artist has become blue chip they are out of most people's price range. Elevation to this status is decided mostly by museum curators, art world big spenders, and investors such as Charles Saatchi. Even so, of the many artists working today only a fraction will become blue chip.

ART SHOULD BE ORIGINAL

Originally artists were nameless. They were the mere labourers involved in creating an altarpiece or painting an icon for Christian worshippers. But those "labourers" with a particular human individuality, however, began to stand out. Although Fra Angelico was painting the same subject matter as every other Renaissance artist, there was a common consensus that his work had a certain something, at the time indefinable to most people because there were not any art critics around in 14th-century Italy. Fra Angelico had an individual style that came from within.

The best artists do not imitate, they learn from what went on before in order to expand their own work.

Another urinal shown as a piece of art (see p.24) will never be worth anything, because Conceptual art is based on an idea that, once expressed, cannot be copied. So much is in a name, too. When Ed Ruscha makes letters out of paper to spell the word "Things" for example, this is worth a lot of money and is worthy of showing in a museum. If Gerhard Richter reproduced a paint chart from a hardware store it would probably fetch £250,000–£350,000 ($450,000–$630,000) at Sotheby's in London. If I, or even a recent art graduate, did the same it would be worth nothing. The best artists should start with a surprise, something that no one else has done before. When their originality has come to the notice of the art establishment and the moniker "artist" is bestowed on them, collectors and art dealers have given them licence to transform the mundane into high art.

Art that reminds you of the work of a famous artist is not a wise investment. It will always be compared to the more famous work and be regarded as an inferior copy. For example, the 1997 exhibition *Sensation* at the Royal Academy, London, launched the careers of British artists such as Damien Hirst and Tracey Emin – it included very few traditional oil-on-canvas works and certainly lived up to its name. The trouble is that for some artists sensationalism seems to be the *raison d'etre* for too much of their work. Continuing in this vein is no longer so effective because it is derivative and unoriginal.

HOW CAN YOU LEARN MORE ABOUT ART?

The old cliché, "I know what I like", is often uttered by the ignorant as a means of stifling any conversations about art, and rarely by people who really do know about what they like. Another maxim that is certainly valid when it comes to buying art is "knowledge is power". Here are a few practical suggestions:

Courses Whether at colleges, universities, or even auction houses – there is a plethora of courses available to suit any interest, level of ability, and level of assessment desired.

Visit museums and exhibitions Of course you are not going to be able to buy the artists shown in the Louvre or the Metropolitan, but looking at the very best teaches you so much. Looking at how a master depicts light and shade, or works with a piece of bronze, will help you to learn about quality. And always remember that no artist starts at the top – every one shown in the top museums started in small galleries or friends' houses, selling their work for peanuts. Knowing what good art is helps you to spot examples in the most unexpected places. Nowadays it is so cheap and easy to get on a plane or train to see the Guggenheim in Bilbao, the Louvre, and other smaller museums and galleries. Take a trip to London or New York and explore their thriving small galleries scene or even visit one of the international biennial art events around the world that showcase new talent.

Read Scour second-hand art bookshops: most have sections with books on individual artists or art movements. Alternatively, look on the book websites for access to second-hand bookstores all over the world. Bookshops in major galleries now also have a comprehensive collection of art books and journals on sale. See the Useful Contacts & Reference throughout the book, and the Bibliography and Periodicals list on pp.188–9.

GOOD ART NEED NOT BE EXPENSIVE

"Art is a lie that enables us to tell the truth," Pablo Picasso once observed. Presumably he was talking about artifice, the creation of an image to illustrate a point. A good work of art should excite you and give you pleasure – whether it's Picasso's *Boy with a Pipe* or a tiny pencil sketch by an unknown Victorian. It is difficult to rationalize and explain what attracts people to a certain painting or sculpture. You should not be affected by price tags, although in reality there is a common consensus on what makes good art, and that can often be reflected in the price. It is a good idea to view pieces in a gallery without looking at the price list. After you have been round the show then look to see if the pieces you like are the most expensive in the show.

HOW DO YOU JUDGE IF A WORK IS GOOD?

You may not be able to say whether you like a picture or a sculpture when you see it, but you can judge if it is technically proficient. Pictures and sculpture have a physical quality that you have to admire. You may not understand or indeed like Jackson Pollock's large drips of paint or the crudely applied oils of Frank Auerbach, for instance, but the painters' use of materials is fascinating. Sculpture has a tactile quality; the subject matter may not appeal, but close your eyes and rub your hands along the surface to appreciate it on another level.

It would be a great mistake to buy a work of art that you didn't even like purely for investment purposes. So when looking at a piece run the following questions through your head:

- **What does this piece of art say to me?**
- **Does it make me smile or feel happy?**
- **Does it ask questions of me, the viewer, and sometimes even make me feel uncomfortable?**
- **Does it inspire me?**
- **Does it stretch my imagination?**
- **Does it make me feel calm and serene?**
- **Is it beautiful?**

All these feelings can be incorporated to some degree in a painting, sculpture, photograph, or any other medium through the use of colour, symmetry, and the message the piece contains (whether it is overt or hidden). The best art, like the best books and theatre, speaks personally to each viewer.

BUYERS' TIP
Don't play safe – it is always those pictures that are well executed but slightly off-beam that become sought after in times to come.

USEFUL CONTACTS & REFERENCE

LEARNING ABOUT ART

Auction house courses Both Christie's and Sotheby's run their own accredited art courses, often attended by those who want a career in the fine art world. They also run a series of evening lectures. Visit www.sothebys.com or call +44 (0)20 7462 3232 (London) / +1 212 894 1111 (New York); or visit www.christies.com or call +44 (0)20 7665 4350 (London) / +1 212 355 1501 (New York). Christie's also have courses in Australia and Paris.

Grove Dictionary of Art Running to 34 volumes, including an index, this is a wonderful all-embracing book. (Macmillan, London, fully updated in 1997).

Liverpool Biennial An international showcase of art held every other autumn in one of Britain's rising cultural centres. Visit www.biennial.com or call +44 (0) 151 709 7444.

The National Art Library This is housed at the Victoria and Albert Museum in London and can be visited in museum opening hours. Membership is free with proof of identification. The library is a wonderful Victorian room, and books can be studied there. You can also search their database online at www.vam.ac.uk, or call +44 (0)20 7942 2400.

The Smithsonian Institute Washington DC's Smithsonian has a very interactive education department, and many websites devoted to different fields of art and science. Visit www.si.edu – there are many different pages on art and you can even ask the experts at the American Art Museum questions by clicking on the Joan of Art icon. Contact by telephone on +1 202 633 1000.

The Westminster Reference Library Located in London's Trafalgar Square, this has a very good collection of art books and periodicals. At the time of going to press the library is open 1–8pm, but check on +44 (0)20 7641 1300 before visiting. To use their photocopiers etc you have to join the library, but you don't have to live in London as long as you have proof of an address in Britain.

Venice Biennale The International Art Exhibition at the Venice Biennale – the oldest and most famous exhibition of contemporary art from around the world – is held every two years in June. Visit www.labiennale.org or call +39 041 5218711.

SECOND-HAND & ANTIQUARIAN BOOK SITES

www.abebooks.com This is by far the largest online bookstore in the world. Prices are given in US dollars but can be converted into local currencies. To find uniquely British bookstores visit www.abebooks.co.uk.

www.bibliopoly.com This European online bookstore can be viewed in English, German, Spanish, and French. Prices are in Euros.

www.bookfinder.com and **addall.com** will search across abe and bibliopoly and compare prices.

www.ilab-lila.com On this website for the International League of Antiquarian Booksellers you may find the rare book you are seeking that sellers might not wish to put on the larger sites.

TRAVEL

www.easyjet.com, www.ryanair.com, www.flybmi.com, www.lastminute.com, www.driveline.co.uk (Driveline Europe: +44 (0)871 222 1008) Sites like these are a good place to start for cheap flights within Europe, with good deals for weekend breaks to cultural cities such as Bilbao, Prague, and Paris.

WHAT TO BUY

"We have to have art or we don't know who we are." Howard Barker

What you will learn in this chapter:

- Key developments in the history of each of the visual arts
- Explanations of the terms used in each field
- Notable exponents and affordable fields to investigate
- Guidelines on what to look out for

At the beginning of the 21st century there is more choice of "art" than ever before – whether in the traditional materials of oils, watercolours, pencil, and pen and ink, or the new emerging media, such as video and digital. This book cannot hope to cover every medium and genre, and that is not its purpose. It has been my aim in this chapter to write about the art that is relevant to us today, highlighting various media and subject matters that have gained in popularity and value, or are just beginning to, or that I feel might increase in value over the coming years.

I am not a fortune teller – the future is always uncertain – but if read in conjunction with other points I make throughout the book, such as what affects the price of art in chapter one, it becomes clear that the areas covered in this chapter are affordable, and in some cases undervalued, and are consequently potential cases for a rise in prices. Any historical detail provided when discussing the various media and genres is intended to refresh your memory, and should in no way be viewed as a substitute for a thorough reading-up on a specific subject that interests you in order to gain a grounding in its background. Please also refer to chapter four, where certain areas are highlighted as being particularly affordable at this time, or are likely to be so soon.

Thus I have been selective. Most people are more likely to hang a 20th-century drawing in their home than a heavy 17th-century Dutch oil landscape. Old portraits are included here because there is currently a taste for mixing old portraits with new furniture in interior design schemes. Victorian landscapes in oil, however, are not included in this chapter as there are just so many, and oil in general is not often an affordable area – although we will see how painting, including oils, is enjoying a resurgence in popularity. Nevertheless, a landscape that has colour, detail, and an atmosphere of climate will always be in demand, particularly as the world becomes more and more suburbanized. In particular, for example, landscape watercolours of the Wild West represent freedom, an escape from the restrictions of modern life. They are an enduring reminder of the origins of the United States and will always be valuable.

Another example of a genre not worth discussing in depth here is sporting art. This rose hugely in price 30 years ago and the best examples are still not affordable. Second-rate sporting art is not relevant to this generation. I have also steered away from Latin American art and paintings from the Far East because these are two vast subjects to which I would not be able to do justice. However, I have included oriental drawings and prints because they have a wide appeal and potential for investment. Graffiti art, although enjoying a renaissance in popularity, is not included as it is very mural-based and therefore not easy to collect.

In every field of art there are a several objective factors that make some pictures more valuable than others. When you are dealing with relatively unknown, and consequently affordable, artists it is important that you bear these in mind. While famous and blue-chip names are discussed, it is merely to show you what qualities to look out for and to encourage you to seek out these qualities in affordable – and often therefore new and emerging – artists. With practice you will eventually train your eye to recognize the signs of universal quality, in addition to the characteristics and content that may also have personal appeal for you.

"DECORATOR ART" VERSUS "DECORATIVE ART"

Beware of chain store galleries with branches in more than one location; they will only sell pictures as accessories to your soft furnishings. This is called "decorator art" and it has been multiplying hugely in the last few years. There is a risk that much of what you will find at the art fairs promoting bargains is decorator art. It has as much resale value as a sequined cushion, i.e. not much. I use the term decorator art because it is contrived to tie in with current trends in wall colours and sofa fabrics.

It must be stressed that many pictures are very decorative, and these are certainly a good investment because there is always a market for attractive paintings. But, unlike decorator art, they have an attractive quality that is original and inherent and stands above interior design taste – in a room, the picture would stand out, not blend in. These works look good now and will continue to do so in a hundred years. Many decorative artists painted in a naïve manner, such as Alfred Wallis – a retired Cornish fisherman who depicted boats and seaside scenes – but they don't contort figures and landscapes to illustrate some inner feeling. What you see is what you get.

It would be wrong to dismiss a large number of decorative painters as mere "Sunday painters". Many, such as the English artist Mary Fedden and the American Mose Tolliver, are represented by galleries and have art school training.

DRAWINGS & SKETCHES

Buying drawings and sketches is an excellent way to start an art collection, as they are generally cheaper than paintings. They are also good investments, because when the price of an artist's paintings rise so do those for his or her works on paper. Drawings and sketches by internationally respected artists can be bought for reasonable prices, so if you want to own something by a famous artist then this can be the way forward. They are also, for the most part, smaller and easy to display in the average house.

In terms of big names, oils by the Impressionists can fetch tens of millions of dollars or even pounds, but a tiny Cézanne pencil landscape of one his favourite areas of France, L'Estaque, sold at auction in Japan in September 2004 for 1,700,000 Japanese yen (that works out at about US$15,540), which is relatively cheap! An oil by a very important French landscape artist who just pre-dated the Impressionists, Jean Corot, can fetch £200,000 ($360,000), but a little sketch by him of some trees can be had for under £1,000 ($1,800). John Constable is one of Britain's most famous artists, and in 2003 a small pencil drawing of Stoke-by-Nayland Church in Suffolk made £11,500 (about $18,400 at the time) at auction. Of course if the picture depicted a more recognizable place in Suffolk, the price would have been higher. Ans Joseph Mallord William Turner drew travellers in a Swiss valley in pencil and wash, a work which sold in 2003 for £6,000 ($9,600).

> **BUYERS' TIP**
> If you choose a subject matter that an artist is not famous for, as a small picture or a work on paper, it is possible to pick up something by a world-famous artist for a relatively reasonable sum.

"OLD MASTER" AND "MASTER" DRAWINGS

The term "Old Master" is rather vague. There is no precise definition, but we commonly refer to European artists working before 1700 as Old Masters. Important Old Masters include Leonardo de Vinci, Rembrandt, Rubens, Raphael, and Titian – the "big league" artists.

When viewing auction house sales entitled "Old Masters", do not expect to see works of museum stature – indeed many of the paintings will be pretty crude and by relatively unknown artists. The sole criterion for their inclusion in the sale is that they should be painted before 1700 and after the Italian Renaissance. Calling these artists "Masters" is flattery, as they tend to merely copy important Old Masters rather badly.

More interesting, in my opinion, and more in tune with contemporary tastes, are Old Master drawings. In our label-obsessed age, an Old Master drawing by an important artist is far more collectable than an inferior Old Master oil painting by a less well-known artist.

There has always been confusion over the term Old Master drawings. In France and the United States Joshua Reynolds could be labelled as an Old Master, and in Britain 18th-century French artists are included in the same category. In New York, 19th-century drawings by Millet and Agasse were also included in a recent Sotheby's Old Masters sale.

In Britain, in order to try and clear up the confusion the term "Master drawings" is now used. This term is used to describe drawings by artists who are considered to be "master artists". They may date from the 20th century or before, but if the are 17th-century or older they are still referred to as Old Masters.

If you want to see how some of the greatest artists worked, study their drawings. Early drawings by German, Italian, Dutch, and French Masters were preliminary sketches for larger works in oil or tempera; they were not intended as works of art to be sold to patrons. The artist would keep them for reference and when he died they would be acquired by other artists for inspiration, and to study his technique.

BUYING GUIDELINES

Preliminary drawings The light monochrome touch of such drawings particularly appeals to modern buyers, often more so than the heavy and melodramatic finished oil paintings on religious or allegorical subjects. It is also fascinating to see the preparatory workings of the Old Masters.

Provenance A number of very special, and therefore valuable, Old Master drawings have been passed from master to master, and have been stamped or inscribed discreetly at an edge or on the back as they have passed down the line. This gives them extra historical interest and provenance (see p.101). The journalist and author Huon Mallalieu has discovered one such line: the 17th-century English portrait painter Sir Peter Lely was a great collector of drawings, and his collection passed to his assistant Prosper Lancrinck, then probably on to portrait painter Thomas Hudson, who passed it on to his pupil Joshua Reynolds.

British drawings These were not just for the artist's use. Gainsborough, Reynolds, and Constable sold their drawings, treating them as works of art in their own right. Certain top quality artists specialized in drawings. As a result, British drawings are among the most accessible and sought after. Continental European artists tended to depict religious and allegorical subjects, which were not always so pretty.

Oil sketches Another affordable area is oil sketches. These were originally used purely as artists' aide-mémoires. Artists who relied on oil sketches included John Constable and his near contemporary James Ward, the animal painter. It is interesting to note that in Ward's sketches of horses moving, he depicts what we now have only relatively recently seen through photography – the correct leg configuration. But maybe this discovery would have been too radical for his clients, and in the oil he stuck to the unnatural, rocking-horse-like stretched legs as seen in the art of John Frederick Herring and John Wootton.

Unattributed drawings An authenticated drawing by Raphael is of course far more desirable to collectors than works by the many artists who might have seen his work and copied it as an exercise. Nevertheless, these pictures, whose catalogue description might be "after so and so", are often very competent and make an attractive purchase; they are relatively inexpensive and look good anywhere. There is a multitude of drawings that cannot be attributed to any artist, original or copied, and these are simply catalogued as, for example, "Bolognese School" or "Dutch School" (*see* Explanation of cataloguing terms, below). They vary enormously in quality, but well-executed examples are worth collecting. They are unique and obviously will become rarer as nature and accidental damage take their toll.

EXPLANATION OF CATALOGUING TERMS

When auction houses are certain that a painting is by Rembrandt, for instance, they will put his name and dates as a caption. However, here is a guide to the various terms that auction houses use in their catalogues when there is not so much certainty:

"Signed", "dated inscribed", "stamped" Terms like these mean that the expert or specialist who has viewed the work is pretty sure that the artist has signed the work himself, although a question mark indicates an element of doubt.

"With stamp", or "with inscription" Many artists have a stamp that may be applied by another, authorized, person.

"Attributed to Rembrandt" When the specialist thinks that the painting is by the artist, but is not sure enough to caption the work with his name alone.

"Workshop of Rembrandt" This indicates that the artist may have had help from another artist in painting the clothing or other minor parts of the painting. It could also mean that the picture was executed by someone else under his supervision, and so was not actually painted by him personally.

"Circle of Rembrandt" This indicates a work done by an artist who was strongly influenced by Rembrandt and who copied his style, without necessarily being his pupil.

"Follower of Rembrandt" This is a bit less specific than "Circle of". The artist painted in Rembrandt's style and lived around the same time or was working soon after the master's death.

"Manner of Rembrandt" This refers to a painter working in the style of Rembrandt but at a later date.

"After Rembrandt" This signifies, in the specialist's opinion, a copy of a known work of the artist.

"School of Rembrandt" Old Master paintings and drawings can often be described as "school of" when the auction house does not know who painted a picture but recognizes similarities with the master or group of masters. The most common schools include: the Bolognese School, which refers to unknown artists working in the Italian city of Bologna and copying the city's famous early 17th-century masters Annibale Carracci and his family, Domenichino, and Guido Reni; the Venetian School, who were followers of Titian, Tintoretto, and Veronese; and the 18th-century Dutch School, characterized by pictures in the style of Old Masters such as Van Huysum or Brueghel.

ORIENTAL DRAWINGS

As I explain in chapter four (How to Get the Best Deals, p.98), while considering what type of art to invest in it is worth buying into the native art of burgeoning economies. I'll talk about Chinese modern art later, but in this section it is definitely worth looking back at oriental drawings from the past 300 years. These will appeal to the ever-increasing market of the affluent Chinese, who thanks to the Internet and mass communication, are now able to buy from outside China.

Space does not allow me to go into great detail here about Chinese and Japanese drawings, but they were masters of calligraphy and used pen and ink on beautiful handmade paper to great effect. Their fine and delicate ink landscapes and depictions of birds, fish, and flowers have a timeless appeal. The Chinese also painted on silk and satin, but to a modern eye their work on paper is preferable. In the West we are most familiar with Japanese prints and woodcuts, which I shall deal with in the print section (see pp.57–8).

During the 17th and 18th centuries the visual arts flourished in China. Up to this time, artists had been expected to paint in a very stylized fashion and the individuality of the artist was not encouraged. With the influx of foreigners and the growth of a rich merchant class this all changed, and the idiosyncrasies of artists came to be regarded as a bonus. Indeed a movement developed known as the Individualists, the most famous and most influential of whom was Zhu Da, also known as Bada Shanren. Also look out for Shi Tao and Dong Quichang.

Experts on Chinese art, such as the writer and curator Mary Tregear, are of the opinion that during the 19th century a period of stylistic stagnation set in, in which technical skill was prized above everything. It was not until the early 20th century, when Chinese artists travelled to Paris to see Matisse and Picasso, that interesting and unique work began to be produced again. Lin Feynman is the most famous artist from that period. Unfortunately Chairman Mao and the Cultural Revolution in the 1940s and 1950s stifled challenging work, although the works produced at that time are interesting to some collectors who are fascinated by the politicization of art. During these times, traditional Chinese art was considered by the authorities to be inaccessible. They wanted didactic art and depictions of heroes of the Revolution. Artists were sent to the other great communist state, Russia, and Russian artists came to China. An example of political art can be seen in the work of Li Keran, who painted a landscape based on a poem by Mao. His style is dark and heavy.

In the 1980s Chinese artists began to suffer less from the ideological demands of the government and were able to paint in a more free and reflective manner, akin to their fellow artists who had emigrated to North America and Europe. Artists such as Ren Rong illustrate well the mix of Chinese and European artistic traditions.

EXPLANATION OF DRAWING TERMS AND MEDIA

Chalk, ink, and wash Old Master drawings were executed in chalk, ink, and wash. They are brown today because the ink has faded to that colour. The pens they used were made from quills or reeds, as metal nibs had not been invented. Chalk was usually black or red and washes were brown and grey, or sometimes blue and grey.

Charcoal This has always been used by artists, but because it can easily wear off paper only more modern examples of charcoal drawings are to be found today.

Conté A wood-encased stick of compressed fired graphite and clay was invented in 1795 by Nicolas Conté. It is harder in appearance than pastel but softer and fuzzier than pencil.

Crayon Pigment and chalk combined with gum and bound in wood was a medium popular with late 19th-century painters such as Henri Toulouse Lautrec and Jacques Villon. In 1903 crayons in the form that we know them today – extruded paper wax crayons – were invented. Composed of high percentages of paraffin and stearic acid, these are now sold to children everywhere because of their ease of use and bold colours. Artists such as Pablo Picasso, Arshile Gorky, and naïve painters used these crayons. Philip Guston used crayon to make simple bold statements.

Pencil These basic drawing tools have not always been made out of the materials we know them to be today. When a picture from the 17th and 18th centuries is described as being in pencil, this refers to a small thin brush. In Victorian times pencils were made from lead; today they are made of graphite.

Pastel Pastel was popular with 15th-century artists. It is similar to crayon, in that is made from the same ingredients, but the combination of the ingredients is different. A pastel finish is much drier and chalkier and less waxy than crayon. The problem with pastel is that, like charcoal, it is difficult to fix, and therefore tends to come off the paper if it is touched.

Cross-hatching This involves vigorous pencil strokes forming intersecting parallel lines across a drawing to give different tonal and shading effects. If you see a drawing divided into squares, on the other hand, this indicates that it has since been made into a print.

WATERCOLOURS

There is a misconception that watercolour painting is for amateurs, fuelled by the fact that few contemporary artists use the medium. However, it was originally far from a dilettante discipline. Indeed, because the materials were easily transportable, an ability to record a landscape in wash and watercolour was a prized attribute in the army, as a soldier could record his travels and illustrate the terrain for others. A gentleman was expected to draw and illustrate in watercolour, and in Russia Peter the Great insisted that everyone should be reasonably accomplished in the art of watercolour, whether they liked it or not. His son, the tsarevich, knew that he had no talent for the art, but rather than face the wrath of his father he shot himself in the hand, so that his misfortune should never be discovered.

The watercolour technique was used by the Ancient Egyptians on papyrus rolls, and on vellum manuscripts in medieval Europe. Dürer skilfully used this medium for its own merits. Rubens and Van Dyck were watercolourists, too, but the technique did not really become fashionable and widespread until the 18th century. The English landscape artists Paul Sandby and J.R. Cozens brought it to the attention of the English aristocracy, and of a great many other English artists.

Photography had not, of course, been developed in the 18th century, so fine artists were sent to reproduce beauty spots or interesting parts of the world and its peoples. Watercolours by British artists turn up in the most unexpected places as a result. They must have been forced to travel light, and so decided to leave some of their surplus watercolours behind. Sometimes their works were left to pay for a night's drinking – inn drawings, for example, were offered as payment to innkeepers.

Two artists revolutionized watercolour art: Thomas Girtin and Joseph Mallord William Turner, both men of extraordinary talent. They advanced the art of watercolour from the level of mere photographic representation, to painting with mood and atmosphere. They daringly did not outline their subjects, as artists had done previously, but painted directly on to the paper. It may be an overstatement to say that they were the first artists to give a feeling of atmosphere, but stylistically they were certainly two of the best, and brought watercolours to the attention of great art collectors. In 1805 the British Watercolour Society was founded, and excellent artists were drawn to the medium, including the likes of John Varley, John Sell Cotman, David Cox, Peter De Wint, Anthony Vandyke Copley Fielding, and William Havell. Watercolours were no longer merely a preparation for, or a quick version of, a painting.

In the 1830s Richard Bonington, Thomas Boys, and William Callow began to accentuate the linear aspect of a drawing with watercolour and not, as was usual at the time, with a pencil or pen. J.S. Cotman used a paste medium to give his pictures body without opacity, dragging it around the picture in a streaky and uneven fashion to give depth and variety. And J. Varley heightened the intensity of his work by applying a varnish of glue.

BUYERS' TIP

Watercolours by members of the British Watercolour Society from the first half of the 19th century are for the most part very good investments. This was a very exciting period for watercolour painting, when many artists were competing to innovate and employ new techniques.

Because watercolours were easily transportable, in the United States all early Wild West and cowboy art was done in watercolour. The major 19th-century American naturalist painter Winslow Homer also worked mainly in watercolour.

The next leap, a stylistic one this time, happened 100 years later in the mid-20th century, in the work of British artists Piper, Bawden, Sutherland, and Ardizzone. Their style was more abstract, more atmospheric, and even less concerned with recording a scene or a place as it looks in real life. John Piper was an official war artist during the Second World War, and also painted a series of English landscapes.

BUYING GUIDELINES

Victorian watercolours There were a great many very competent mid-Victorian watercolour artists, and if you look back at price lists of auctions from the 1970s they seem to have been ridiculously cheap by today's standards. However, if you take into account inflation and wage rises in the past 30 years, they have not risen in value as much as you might think, and probably will not do so in the future. This is mainly because there were just so many amateurs and professionals in this field. Nevertheless, if you are considering collecting Victorian watercolours, a view of a beauty spot or tourist attraction will always be more valuable than an unrecognizable scene. The big names, such as Edward Lear and John Ruskin, are greatly appreciated by collectors and will always hold their value.

Shell Collection Particularly interesting are watercolours commissioned by Shell Oil for a series of travel and nature guides in the years just after the Second World War. The company sold off this collection of fine botanic drawings by excellent British artists such as Tristram Hillier, landscapes by Rowland and Edith Hilder, still lifes by John Armstrong, and many others, in 2003. To find out more about these watercolours it is worth contacting Sotheby's to see if they have any back catalogues of the Shell artists sale. Prices for the Shell artists are in the low thousands with some even lower (work from the 1960s is often cheaper than earlier works), but these minutely detailed watercolours are becoming very fashionable and could well rise in value.

American and cowboy art A book published nearly 40 years ago declared that cowboy pictures were not worth buying because they were too expensive. Buyers ignored this advice, and cowboy art keeps on rising in price. It will probably continue to do so, as cowboys are so much a part of American history. Paintings by the well-known American landscape artist Winslow Homer are extremely expensive because of the places they depict – in many cases the same landscape is radically different today. If you are interested in buying American watercolours, be aware that views of famous places that look very different today, even by less expensive artists than Winslow Homer, are still very much worth collecting because they have a historical value. However, a general point to remember is that, by and large, European watercolours are cheaper than American ones because there are so many more of them.

Individuality Look for this quality as it is this that makes the likes of Turner and his immediate successors worth buying. The same can be said for Piper, Bawden, and Sutherland, whose prices were low a few years ago but are now rising.

Early English pen-and-wash drawings These are a hybrid of two media, but are well worth buying. They are not collected by watercolour or drawing purists, but have an affordable charm that more and more people are beginning to appreciate.

EXPLANATION OF WATERCOLOUR TERMS

Body colour Describes a watercolour that has been made opaque by the addition of chalks or white calcium carbonate and a binding agent such as gum or honey. When body colour is added, those in the trade call it "heightening". When used over the entire picture, rather than just for emphasis, the watercolour becomes a gouache.

Gouache A watercolour given body and an opaque quality by the addition of a chalky white powder, usually calcium carbonate. This term was used in France in the 18th century but was not adopted by the English until the 1880s.

Pen and wash Outlines drawn in pen are washed over with much-diluted watercolour paint, mostly brown, grey, or blue, to give line drawings depth.

Tempera This was used before the advent of oil painting and is still sometimes used today. It consists of colour pigments ground in egg yolk diluted with water so that it is easy to apply.

WAYS OF DESCRIBING SUBJECT MATTER

Abstract Non-representational arrangement of patterns to create a desired effect, sometimes evocative of recognizable forms, but not delineating them in a clear or realistic manner.

Allegorical Representing a myth, legend, or parable from the Bible or Ancient Greece or Rome. Characters and motifs in these pictures serve as symbols to illustrate the story.

Figurative Used to describe pictures with comprehensible images, as opposed to abstract paintings in which the images are not easily recognizable.

Genre Depicting scenes from everyday life for its own sake; the people or things in the paintings have no allegorical significance.

Representational Featuring recognizable images found in the objective world or in the artist's imagination. A reasonably faithful portrait is an example of representational art .

PORTRAITS

Some of the finest British and American artists have been portrait painters – Gainsborough and Sargent spring immediately to mind. Portraiture was very lucrative before photography became the common way of taking likenesses. Painters were commissioned regularly to paint images of people, and it seems we still love a good portrait, as they account for a third of all paintings sold in Britain.

Landowners, government officials, and businessmen commissioned portraits of themselves and their families to hang in their mansions, often showing them in all their finery and in a grand setting, by a classical pillar or in front of their country houses. These pictures are known as "swagger" portraits.

BUYING GUIDELINES

Swagger portraits There exist countless swagger portraits from the last 300 years: many are not very good, but others can fetch large sums. It is, however, possible to buy swagger portraits by well-known artists, such as Joshua Reynolds, for around £5,000 ($9,000), but only if the subject is unknown. Unsurprisingly, a famous sitter by this artist could fetch £250,000 ($450,000) – a portrait of a famous person for the most part sells better than that of an unknown.

However, an unknown who is beautiful or handsome will always captivate future generations and carry a price premium. For example, a 60-year-old, bewhiskered, Victorian town councillor in front of the town hall would not be nearly as saleable as an alluringly dressed 20-year-old girl!

On a more affordable level, mid-20th-century swagger portraits are now coming up for sale and many are extremely well done. By the middle of the 20th century portrait painters were taking more risks, often to the displeasure of their patrons, who only wanted pictures of themselves in the most flattering light. Winston Churchill, for example, so disliked a Graham Sutherland portrait of him that he destroyed it. Sutherland has been much undervalued in the last 30 years, but prices for his work are now beginning to climb.

Genealogy Art dealer Philip Mould has made a good business out of tracing family portraits, so if by chance you have a portrait of a member of the British aristocracy or of a Victorian called Gates who could be an ancestor of Bill, it could be worth contacting Historical Portraits Ltd in London (see Useful Reference p.92).

Conversation pieces Sentimental, moralizing Victorian portraits are not fashionable at the moment unless they are by a famous artist. More interesting are what is known in the trade as "conversation pieces", which depict a family together. A good conversation piece should make the viewer curious about the subjects: what were the sitters doing before, and how did their lives turn out after, the painting? Who was having an illicit affair with whom? Were the parents kind or cruel? Does it show in the picture? A good conversation piece should be like a freeze-frame from a soap opera.

William Orpen and Irish portraits We all love sex and intrigue, whether on television or on a canvas. One portrait painter who expressed this in a sophisticated and exciting way was the Irish portrait painter Sir William Orpen. Active at the end of the 19th century, he painted the Irish and Anglo-Irish gentry. One of his subjects was a lady called Mrs St George, with whom he had an affair. One memorable picture depicts her in flushed abandon, as if she has just been, or about to be, intimate with Orpen. The picture is not smutty or obvious, but rather passionate in its formality, especially as St George was already married. She is lounging on a chair fully clothed, but it is the look on her face and the way she is sitting, in luxurious abandon, that tells us what is, or has been, going on. This picture, entitled *Interior at Clonsilla with Mrs St George,* fetched £1 million ($1.8 million) – four times as much as any other portrait of his. Any Orpen portrait is therefore not "cheap", so it might be a good idea to look instead at the work of Sir John Lavery. Interesting Laverys sell in Ireland for over €50,000 (£34,000/$61,000), although many sell for half of that, and his watercolours for under €3,000 (£2,000/$3,600).

There are excellent, less expensive Irish artists whose portraits are good investments, such as Robert Ballagh, now in his 60s and known in some circles as the "Irish Andy Warhol". Work by him can be bought for €3,000–10,000 (£2,000–7,000/$3,600–13,000). James Hanley is another. Secretary of the Royal Hibernian Academy, he paints in a photorealist style. His prices range from €2,000 (£1,300/$2,500) to €5,000 (£3,400/$6,500). Incidentally, any Irish work of art these days is climbing in value, thanks to the dynamism of the Irish economy in the last decade. Crumbling mansions are being lovingly restored by new owners, who are looking for pictures to put on their walls.

English Victorian portraits This market goes up and down regularly, so it is only the best quality examples that are a good investment. There are just so many portraits from this time, so look for good-looking subjects, a good rendition of clothing, or a famous figure. For example, a couple I know have what they believe to be a very rare picture of Jane Austen. The picture is not particularly good, the artist unknown, but the subject matter is of enormous interest so would command a high price if authenticated. Glamour and mystery also make portraits interesting. Sargent usually painted rich society people, but in a private collection there exists a picture by him of a young handsome urchin. Art historians and Sargent collectors are transfixed by this picture because it is so different from his other work, and was apparently executed without any thought for the huge pay cheque that could be earned from a wealthy patron.

Late Tudor and Stuart portraits Portraits done during the reigns of these two dynasties at the end of the 16th century and the beginning of the 17th century rarely have the informality of a good conversation piece – the subjects are always posed very stiffly without any expression, and often with a castle or large house behind them to show their status – but they are fascinating in a different way. It is difficult not to be drawn in by what we know of the British aristocracy of this time – the history of their lives, the intrigue, the plotting, and their perilous existence, dependent on the whim of their sovereigns. Considering all this history, some of these pictures, mostly catalogued as "circle of" (see p.41), can be had for under £5,000 ($9,000). There were then fewer artists working under their own name than there are today, so many good circle of William Segar or Marcus Gheeraerts come up for sale. Good circle of Gheeraerts portraits can fetch £30,000 ($54,000).

The two big names of the period, Sir Peter Lely and Sir Godfrey Kneller, employed a number of artists to help them, and there are therefore many works attributed to Kneller and Lely. As mentioned previously, high prices are reached when the sitter is famous. A portrait of a lady said to be Nell Gwynn, by Sir Peter Lely, fetched £65,000 ($117,000) at Sotheby's recently. By contrast, another picture by Lely merely described as "portrait of a lady, three-quarter length, in a grey dress and mauve wrap" fetched £12,300 ($19,500) at Christie's, London in 2000. However, a portrait by this artist of a not particularly attractive baronet will sell for only around £3,000 ($5,400).

"Circle of" Many picture sales have portraits that are catalogued "Circle of" an artist (*see* Explanation of Cataloguing Terms, p.41). This is particularly common with portraits because, just like today, relatives often also wanted copies of the picture. So, before photographic reproduction was possible, various artists in the master's studio would have copied the portraits for him. Masters such as Van Dyck were far too busy to duplicate work; indeed at the height of his popularity he probably only painted the hands and face of a patron, while the rest of the body would have been done by his able assistants.

When buying a replica portrait, look for quality and coherence: for example, does the head tie in well with the body? If there is hard documentary evidence that a replica portrait was requested by another member of the family around the time the original was painted, it is more likely that the master artist would have seen the picture and approved it. Therefore the picture will be of greater value than one that was made after the master's death.

OIL & THE REVIVAL OF PAINTING

As has already been mentioned, traditional oil painting is not a very appropriate (or even appealing) area for people looking to start a collection of affordable art, so there is no need to dwell on it in too much depth here. In the last decade or so of the 20th century the art scene all over the world seemed to be dominated by works in every medium – from readymade sculpture to video art – except paint, namely oil (or its more modern alternatives such as acrylic), on canvas. With some notable exceptions, new artists were not interested in using this medium. Critics wrote about pickled sharks and unmade beds, and curators and dealers preferred to buy Minimalist sculptures by Donald Judd, clay figures by Jeff Koons, or the photographs of Nan Goldin. In a survey of artists commissioned in Britain in 2005 by the *Guardian* newspaper, many curators, critics, and dealers voted Duchamp's urinal the most influential piece of modern art, above the work of Picasso and Matisse. It was Duchamp in 1912 who first claimed that painting was dead because it was only an optical sensation. He was going to give up painting and make different forms of art that challenged the intellect. Since then, there have been many other similar proclamations. Nicholas Serota, Director of the Tate since 1988, commented on this trend in an introduction to *A New Spirit in Painting*, an exhibition that he co-organized at the Royal Academy in 1981: "We are in a period when it seems to many that painting has lost its relevance as one of the highest and most eloquent forms of artistic expression." He went on to defend painting, which is indeed far from dead today: some say that it has been reborn, others that it never died.

The act of painting is one of our basic instincts, and it is clearly ludicrous to claim that it will be superseded by other forms of art such as photography and video art. In the last century painting went in and out of fashion because there were so many other media for artists to work in. Now, after a period of immediate impact art in the form of mixed-media collages, oil paintings are exciting collectors again. Many believe painting has the ability to engage beyond the purely witty and apposite comment, a criticism levelled at some mixed-media contemporary art. Big names include Neo Rauch and his contemporaries in Leipzig, Germany, the Berlin painter Thomas Scheibitz, and Peter Doig, all of whom have international appeal. Neo Rauch created a storm in New York at the Armory Show in 1999. Critics raved, and Ben Lewis, presenter of BBC4's *Art Safari*, wrote in a recent issue of *Prospect Magazine*: "Rauch's clever paintings look as if they borrow other styles of popular illustrations and the colours of interior design books from the 1950s. They are figurative and look allegorical [*see* Ways of

Describing Subject Matter, p.48], but are hard to interpret."
Lewis feels that "the subtle architectural canvases recall the
work of the 1950s artists Graham Sutherland and John Piper".

Not only is paint now the medium of choice for many
contemporary artists, but figurative work is also interesting
collectors once more, after nearly 50 years of abstract art
ruling the roost. So many of the great artists of the 20th
century either produced abstract work or distorted reality. Such
artists include Jackson Pollock and many other American artists,
along with Picasso and all of the Cubists, of course. One of
London's most cutting-edge galleries, Haunch of Venison,
known for video art and installation pieces, is now also
showing figurative painters. Charles Saatchi is also certainly
in agreement, with his 2005, year-long, three-part exhibition
entitled *The Triumph of Painting*.

OIL AND PAINTING TERMS EXPLAINED

Academy board A board prepared for oil painting with white oil-
based ground.

Acrylic A synthetic emulsion used by many 1960s artists. Some
artists during this period did not fix the paint properly and it is now
peeling off. Invented by Otto Rohm in the 1880s and patented in
1915, it was first used in the plastics industry, but Mexican muralists
experimented with it during the 1920s. Jackson Pollock was one of
the most famous artists to experiment with this new material and
helped to popularize it.

Board Catalogue descriptions sometimes say oil on board. A board
is usually made from compressed layers of paper glued together.

Canvas board Canvas pasted on to stiff card, as opposed to being
stretched across a frame.

Cartoon As well as a newspaper or comic strip, the term "cartoon"
can refer to a full-scale drawing used as the rough draft for a
finished oil painting or mural. The most famous in Britain are the
Raphael cartoons in the Victoria and Albert Museum, London.

Sketch A sketch is a preliminary preparatory drawing or painting for
a larger finished work.

> **Study** A study is a detail of a larger work, perhaps of a figure or piece of landscape. It is not sketchy but carefully drawn.

BUYING GUIDELINES

Figurative painting The artists mentioned in this section show in the world's foremost galleries and obviously fetch high prices. However, the fact that these galleries show figurative work will encourage dealers to find figurative artists at a more affordable level too.

Fashion There are thousands of bad pictures cluttering up the auction houses of the world, but there are also good, well-known artists at reasonable prices, who just don't happen to be what the movers and shakers – a tiny number of people in the art world – are into right now.

Relevance and vision Whether you like oil paint thickly or finely applied, choose a piece that has something to say to you as a person in the 21st century. A dreary Victorian landscape or a heavily varnished Dutch scene is so distant from most of our lives today. If you like landscape, for example, it must express the individuality of the painter – it is the painter's vision that makes it so interesting.

Originality Oil paintings that slavishly copy a master are boring and valueless. Cézanne was a master, for example, and there are too many poor imitators of his work.

PRINTS

Prints are generally far more affordable than oil paintings and watercolours. This means that they are a very good and inexpensive way of starting a rewarding art collection. However, there is also a lot to be learned about the subject. Perhaps surprisingly, one print can differ wildly from another, which means one image can be worth a fortune while another, which on first glance looks the same, is valueless.

Artists have made prints of their work since the 15th century, and they can still be bought today without breaking the bank. For example, a woodcut by Albrecht Dürer from 1504 can be bought for under £3,000 ($5,400), and a Rembrandt etching for £1,500 ($2,700). Of course some Dürer prints fetch £60,000 ($110,000), so there are many factors that determine a price.

The best artists of the 20th century in Europe and the United States loved making images specifically for printing – Picasso, Matisse, Warhol, Lichtenstein, Hockney, and Hirst to name but a few. Most are colour lithographs or screen prints (see Printing Terms Explained, pp.60–3) and cost a fraction of a painting by one of these masters, even though prices can reach heights that few of us can aspire to (see the box opposite). In a recent Sotheby's New York print sale, prices for Picasso prints ranged from $3,000 (£1,600) to $80,000 (£45,000), Matisse from $8,000 (£4,500) to $50,000 (£27,000), and Warhol from $3,000 (£1,600) to $80,000 (£45,000). Prints by Lichtenstein and Hockney could be had for under $10,000 (£5,500), and Hirst prints for under $5,000 (£2,700). Lithographs by living artists and good artists working in the last 40 years are even cheaper and will probably rise in price. For example, 1960s artists such as Sam Francis are now becoming collectable. His colourful lithos start at under £1,000 ($1,800).

Established at the end of the 19th century, the Whitechapel Gallery was a charity to bring art to the East End of London – it was the first place to show Picasso in England, for instance. Top contemporary British artists, such as Anish Kapoor, Alex Gordon, and Francis Alys, among others, make prints for the gallery each year, which the Whitechapel sells to fund its work in the local community. These prints, signed by the artists in limited editions of 100 to 500, are a very good investment. Most are priced at £75 ($135) each, and already some from a few years back are fetching four times that each. Indeed a Mark Wallinger print for the Whitechapel Gallery, originally for sale at £75 a couple of years back, could now cost £2,000 ($3,600).

EXPLANATION OF AUCTION CATALOGUE ENTRIES

A Toulouse Lautrec print for sale in New York in 2004 was described as follows: "Lithograph printed in blue, turquoise, and green. 1895. The first state (of three) on wove paper with margins in good condition except for a short repaired tear. Estimate $5,000 –$7,000 [£2,700–3,800]." This picture has margins, which is good and shows that it hasn't been ripped out of a book – margins make a print more valuable. The first state in this instance might not be the best and the damage also makes it less expensive.

Also up for sale in 2004 was Pablo Picasso's *La Suite Vollard*, "the rare complete set of 100 etchings, aquatints, and drypoints. 1930 to 1937. On Montval paper, watermark Picasso or Vollard with full margins, occasional very pale discolouration towards the extreme sheet edges, in very good condition. Estimate £500,000 to £700,000 [$900,000 to $1,260,000]." Christie's in London justify this asking price for the following reasons: "*La Suite Vollard* is a major landmark of Picasso's long and fertile print-making career. Not only is it monumental in scope, with 100 etchings produced over seven years, it is also a fascinating insight into his inspiration and obsessions as the artist approached late middle age." It is incredible that this set should have survived intact and together.

An Andy Warhol screen print of Marilyn Monroe up for auction was catalogued as, "in colour, 1967. On wove paper from the set of ten signed in pencil on the reverse, published by Factory Editions, New York. A minor crease in the lower left of the subject, some slight wear at the tips of the sheet corners, a few spots of old adhesive including one partly on the numbering. Estimate £15,000–£25,000 [$27,000–$45,000]." Marilyn Monroe is an iconic Warhol image, which raises its estimate above £10,000 ($18,000) and in much better condition it would be worth double.

JAPANESE PRINTS

Woodblock printing was practised most notably by the Japanese, and has had worldwide influence, particularly on artists working at the turn of the 18th and 19th centuries. They were responding to the invention of multi-block printing, perfected in the 1740s. Each colour in an image required a separate block that had to be precisely set out, creating a sharp and linear effect.

The woodblock prints of early 19th century Japanese artist Katsushika Hokusai are world famous – his views of Mount Fuji particularly so, so if offered one make sure you snap it up. Kitagawa Utamaro, a generation before him, produced prints of coquettish women and courtesans. These prints were a great influence on the work of Toulouse Lautrec, and to many collectors they are very desirable.

There have been many reproductions of the work of Ando Hiroshige, who perfected a new type of travelogue print, the *Fifty-Three Stages of the Tokaido Highway* being one of the most famous series. Extreme caution must be exercised to ensure that you don't end up with one of the many copies. The "Buying Guidelines" below and opposite give you some of the points you should check before making your purchase

A 20th-century print-maker of international renown was Munakata Shiko, who lived from 1905 to 1977. Towards the end of his life he produced woodblock prints only, often working in monochrome. He also rejected the multimedia printing techniques that were fashionable with Japanese artists of the time. His work from this period is therefore very striking.

BUYING GUIDELINES

Authentic prints It is important to make the distinction between a print, such as a lithograph or a screen print, and something that is simply a photographic reproduction of a painting. You will find hundreds of thousands of these reproductions on the Internet, calling themselves prints. They are worthless and to be avoided. A valuable print must be signed or dated by the artist, or stamped by his or her estate or a print-maker authorized by the artist – a signed print will always be more valuable than a stamped one. It must also be part of a limited edition of one to 100, or perhaps a larger print run. Normally this will be written on the work. Where the print comes in the print run makes no difference to its value: number five is not worth more than number 50, for example. However, when galleries issue prints they often charge more for the last prints in the run because demand may exceed supply by the end.

Where to buy It is important to buy prints from reputable sources. It is in a good gallery's interest to control the supply of prints in order to retain their value.

Condition This is a very important criterion. Prints vary in value, like all works of art, depending on condition. A torn or foxed print will never be as valuable as one in mint condition (foxing occurs when iron deposits in the paper react with damp, creating rust marks). A Rembrandt for, say, £1,500 ($2,700) can generally be expected to have a small tear or a rust mark.

Watermarks and paper Examine the print for a watermark – these do not appear on photocopies. A print will be more valuable if the paper maker can be identified through the watermark. Photocopying is of a high standard today, but fortunately not quite good enough to look old – it cannot mimic 18th-century paper in either weight or texture.

State Another important factor is what is known in the trade as "state". Which state was the print? The first state is the artist's original print. He or she then makes a later state if he or she feels that an improvement or change should be made to the original. It would be an inaccurate generalization to say that the original state is the most desired. This also depends on the artist. In some cases the original is best, with later states being overworked, but in others the later states may represent an improvement. In most cases, however, the last state is the most common, and consequently worth less.

Rarity A print is valuable if it is scarce. Most good print-makers produce editions of 50 to 100.

PRINTING TERMS EXPLAINED

A good way of recognizing good-quality prints is to understand
how they were made and when the various techniques were
invented. Ensure that the print you buy is produced by one of
the methods described below:

Aquatint Like etching (see below), aquatint is an acid-based
process. A layer of bitumen dust is laid on a copper plate, which
is then heated. This causes the dust to adhere to its surface, and
when the plate is immersed in acid, the acid attacks the copper
around each grain of dust, thereby creating a fine web of thin
lines. The technique is particularly suited to imitating areas of
tone, such as those found in watercolour washes. It was invented
in France in the 1760s.

Drypoint The image is scratched onto the plate surface with a
sharp needle. Depending on the force and angle used, fine, sharp
pieces of metal are thrown up on either side of the line. This burr
holds ink, as does the furrow created by the needle, and the result
is a warm, almost blurred line. The greatest exponent of this printing
method was Rembrandt.

Engraving A cutting tool, or burin, is used to cut out thin,
V-shaped furrows from a metal plate. The ink is forced into these
grooves with a roller to produce the image. Tone and shadow can
be created by cross-hatching or a series of fine lines.

Etching This is similar to engraving, but acid is used to remove the
metal rather than a cutting tool. It is one of the earliest print-making
methods. Armour in the 14th century was decorated using the
etching process. A sheet of copper is covered with a wax film and
the image drawn through it with a needle. When dipped in acid,
only the exposed lines are bitten into (as the rest of the plate is
protected by the wax). This tends to produce a more fluid, less
hard-edged line than engraving.

Intaglio This is Italian for engraving. Aquatint, engraving,
etching (including soft-ground etching), drypoint, and mezzotint
are collectively termed intaglio because in all five methods the
image is held in marks made in a printing surface. A characteristic of
intaglio prints is the platemark, an impressed mark around the
image, which is caused by the plate and paper being forced together
in the printing press.

Lithograph The lithography process is based on the principle that water and grease repel each other. The printer draws his design in a greasy medium on a surface covered with water. The surface is then rolled with a greasy printing ink, which will stick to the drawn marks and not the damp areas. Picasso, Toulouse Lautrec, and many early 20th-century artists enjoyed making lithographs.

Mezzotint Italian, meaning "half-tint". A plate is roughened with a fine-toothed tool, known as a mezzotint rocker. When inked, this surface prints a rich, velvety black. The image is created by smoothing (burnishing) areas to produce lighter tones. The process is unusual, therefore, in that it creates a white image from a black background.

Monotype When a picture is painted on a flat sheet of glass and a sheet of paper is then pressed on it this is known as a monotype. G.B. Castiglione invented the process in 1642, and famous exponents of the technique were William Blake and Edward Degas. Many modern artists like to use this technique.

Oleograph Invented in the 19th century to make a print look more like an oil painting. An ordinary colour lithograph was varnished and impressed with a canvas grain.

Pochoir This is the French for stencil. The term is often used in association with Matisse prints.

Proofs In the process of finishing a plate an artist will often print an intermediate or trial proof to see how the image is developing. Where the image is complete, but before publication details have been added, we use the term "proof before letters". A "scratch-letter proof" is where the title and publication details have been lightly scratched in before being engraved. An "artist's proof" is a first impression signed or initialled AP, or EA (for the French, Épreuve d'Artiste), by the artist. It is not counted as part of a limited edition but is additional to it. Although started in the 19th century, this practice did not become widespread until the 1900s. An artist's proof is only more valuable when it differs from the finished edition. If the artist's proof shows the creative process that went into achieving the finished work then it has greater value.

Recto Front of a page that is printed on both sides. **Verso** is the back.

Remarque This was originally a sketch made by an artist in the margin of an etched plate and often unrelated to the main composition. The purpose of such sketches was to test the strength of the acid used in etching. The artist and printer did not want to do this on the main work. Remarque prints were mostly burnished out before the final edition. However a market in remarque proofs grew up in the 19th century for those who could not afford the rare print itself.

Screen printing Gauze of silk, nylon, metal mesh, or, most commonly, silk is stretched tight over a wooden frame. Paper stencils are attached to the underside of the frame. Printing ink is forced through from the top of the frame with a rubber blade to cover the exposed area. Each colour requires a different screen. As well as blocking areas with stencils the screen can be painted out instead. Screen printing is a 20th-century art form, with American artists particularly partial to it. In the 1960s photo stencils were invented, allowing artists to incorporate photographic images.

Soft-ground etching An 18th-century variant of etching where a soft ground, a mixture of ordinary etching ground and tallow, is laid on the metal plate. The artist draws onto a piece of paper that has been laid down on top of the ground. Under the pressure of the pencil the wax sticks to the underside of the paper and pulls away when the paper is lifted. The resulting "marked" plate is placed in an acid bath, where the acid bites into the more exposed areas where the ground has been lifted. The line created is often soft and grainy. The effect is an imitation of a pencil or chalk drawing.

State The number of states refers to the number of times an artist has altered the original. For example if an image is engraved, and subsequently modified four times, the image exists in five versions or "states".

Stipple engraving This is related in function and technique to etching and soft-ground etching. The artist uses a small hammer head covered with tiny points to punch holes in the wax layer (or in some cases directly on the plate). Like soft-ground etching, stipple engraving is used primarily to mimic drawings in chalk and pastel.

Woodcut/Woodblock In this process a design is drawn on a wooden block, and the excess cut away along the grain. The white areas of the design are cut away so that the areas to be printed black are left in relief. Ink is applied with a dabber or roller, then paper is placed on top and pressed to receive the design. This is one of the earliest forms of printing, used as far back as the 12th century to print designs on cloth and textiles. It was used with paper for a further 200 years. Linocuts are a more modern adaptation and are made in the same way, linoleum being substituted for wood. British artists of the mid-20th century, such as Claude Flight and Sybil Andrews, made linocuts popular.

Wood engraving As woodcuts were often rather coarse in texture, the process was refined in the 19th century with the development of wood engraving. In this method, harder woods such as box and pear are cut across the end of the grain and polished. The image is incised with a burin. The result is a cleaner, finer image.

PHOTOGRAPHS

Collecting photographs is one of the fastest-growing areas in the visual arts, and new galleries and fairs are opening all the time, eager to attract clients.

Although photography was invented over 150 years ago, it was not until the end of the 20th century that prices started to go sky high for some photographers' work. For example, 50 years ago you could pick up two of the biggest Victorian names, Julia Margaret Cameron and Lewis Carroll, for a few pence, and in the 1980s it was possible to find very good 19th- and early 20th-century photographs in junk shops and in provincial auctions as part of a job lot. When *The Daily Telegraph* moved from its site in Fleet Street to London Docklands in the early 1980s old photographs of people that had appeared in the newspaper were just chucked into the garbage. One journalist decided to sift through the rubbish and rescued some photographs of Winston Churchill inspecting the troops in the First World War. When sold recently these images fetched £16,500 ($29,700). Also recently, a collector paid the highest figure ever achieved for a photograph – £565,000 ($1,017,000) – by the hitherto unknown French traveller and amateur Joseph-Philibert Girault de Prangey, showing the

Acropolis in Athens in the early 19th century. In the world of painting and sculpture it is big names that fetch the highest prices, but this daguerreotype was surprisingly not by one of photography's big names. Its importance lies in what experts call its "object quality".

Photographs are appraised in two categories, the object quality and image quality. Christie's expert Salome Mitchell believes that the high price paid for the Joseph-Philbert Girault de Prangey was due to its object quality. This very early picture was silver printed on copper daguerreotype. It is not a scrap of paper. It has weight and can be picked up and held. 20th-century photographs, on the other hand, have an image quality. They are valued on printing date, the name of the photographer, and the image depicted. For example the tiny, scrappy 5 x 8cm (2 x 3in) print of Mondrian's studio by Kertesz that was printed immediately after he unloaded his camera, 80 years ago, would be worth in excess of £100,000 ($180,000) today. This is because it is the artist's own print, actually held by him. The same image printed in large glossy format in the 1980s, stamped and printed with permission of Kertesz or his estate, would be worth £2,000–5,000 ($3,600–9,000) depending on the subject matter of the image.

BUYERS' TIP

Most photographs are inexpensive so, if you don't have a huge disposable income, purchasing interesting and original photographs is a good way to start buying art.

WHY ARE PHOTOGRAPHS VALUABLE WHEN YOU CAN REPRODUCE THEM ENDLESSLY?

This is because 19th-century photographs can never be copied authentically, as they were printed entirely differently. Negatives were glass plates, and the same photosensitive paper is unobtainable today. If a modern paper were used, it would be an obvious contemporary reproduction. Glass negatives are also collected, but they are not as valuable as the original prints, because theoretically they could be used to reproduce new images. Even if photographs have been taken using modern techniques, a print can still be valuable if you know it is an original print by the photographer.

PHOTOGRAPHIC PORTRAITS

Hollywood photographs fall into two categories: stars taken by a big name, and intimate portraits of stars taken off duty. Work by Cecil Beaton, Irving Penn, or Annie Liebowitz is valuable thanks to the photographer's reputation rather than the star's position. Of course, A-list stars sell better than bit-part actors on TV shows, but then in reality it is unlikely that Beaton or Penn would have taken photos of them anyway – so there is usually a combination of photographic reputation and star status. For example, Mario Testino took some of the last pictures of Princess Diana before she died. Mario Testino is a distinguished photographer and Princess Diana was very famous and no longer with us, so an original print owned by Mario Testino will be worth a great deal in years to come, although at the moment such an image is not for sale.

In many cases, intimate photographs of stars by less well-known photographers are not as valuable as work by a famous one. A collection of snaps of off-duty Hollywood stars by the photographer Frank Worth, a professional but not in the top-league, has recently come to light. These images are being sold on the Internet in a limited edition of 275 prints. They have fan appeal, but are unlikely to increase substantially in value because they are contemporary and not the original photographer's prints.

Informal snaps of stars taken before they were famous by friends, on the other hand, are greatly sought after today. "If a picture of John Lennon taken by a friend in his student days – there are some around but they are very rare – were offered for sale, it would fetch six figures," says auction house expert Stephen Maycock. Prominent figures, such as the Beatles, John F. Kennedy, and Marilyn Monroe, are A-list material, and photos of them will always sell.

Just as collectable are images made by top photographers of ordinary people. A print that was actually developed by the photographer Irving Penn of a farmhand is very valuable, as is an original print by Diane Arbus of a Coney Island character. An Irving Penn print of a South American farmer from 1948 sold in 2004 for $74,000 (£41,000), a figure that was $14,000 (£7,700) above the top estimate.

BUYERS' TIP

Images that have been featured in books and monographs have an extra cachet.

PHOTOGRAPHIC TERMS EXPLAINED

Albumen print 1851–80s (some use up to early 1910s). Invented by Louis Blanquart-Evrard in 1850. A photographic printing paper coated with salted egg white (albumen) and sensitized with a silver nitrate. The photograph is produced by contact printing in daylight. Albumen prints have a thin paper base and a smooth finish with a light sheen. The image colour ranges from warm brown to purplish-black.

Calotype 1840. Invented by Fox Talbot, this process involves applying gallic acid (developing fluid) to light-sensitive, salted paper.

Daguerreotype 1839–50s. Although first developed in the late 1820s by J.N. Nièpre, this process was not perfected until the late 1830s by Louis Jacques Mande Daguerre. This direct positive process produces a unique image on a silver-plated copper plate. The plate is thoroughly polished, then sensitized with potassium iodide. Once exposed in a camera, the faint or latent image is developed out with mercury fumes. The image can subsequently be intensified and stabilized by toning with gold chloride. Its most distinctive characteristic is the highly reflective silver surface.

Gelatin-silver print 1890s–present day. In the 1880s various formulae for gelatin-silver printing papers were developed from early research by R.L. Maddox in the 1870s. An acetate film or resin-coated paper is coated with a layer of gelatin incorporating light-sensitive silver bromide or silver chloride. Commercial gelatin papers come in a variety of finishes, from glossy to matt, and a range of image colours from warm brown to blue-black – with further alterations of colours through toning. This is how black-and-white prints are made today from negatives, as this process renders the most durable and long lasting photographic print.

Oil process 1904–30s. Invented by G.E. Rawlins in 1904, this is a photograph created in oily ink on gelatin-coated paper. The gelatin is sensitized with potassium bichromate, and then contact-printed in daylight. The bichromate hardens the gelatin in proportion to the exposure. The paper is then inked up and printed. The trouble with this method was that you could only print a picture the same size as the negative. In 1911, Robert Demachy in France and E. Wall in England introduced an oil transfer process enabling a large image to be transferred from a small negative. This needed "bromoil"-coated paper. The Bromoil transfer process was popular until after the Second World War.

Photogram A unique photographic print popular in the early 20th century, made without a camera. Objects are placed on a light-sensitive surface and exposed to light. The objects appear as negative silhouettes. This technique is commonly associated with the work of Christian Schad. British-born Susan Derges creates photograms today. She leaves photographic paper in a landscape or seaside location. Shadows of trees and clouds and maybe a bird flying overhead print themselves on to the paper.

Photogravure 1879–present day. This photo-mechanical process produces a fine, random-grain image in ink, similar in appearance to an aquatint (see p.60). A copper plate is covered with a bichromated carbon tissue and contact-printed in daylight to harden the tissue selectively. The coating is washed to remove the unexposed areas, and the plate dusted with aquatint resin. The plate is then etched to produce a relief image, inked, and printed.

Platinum print 1890–1920s, revived 1970s. Invented by William Willis in 1873 from earlier work by John Herschel, this process produces very stable images. A light-sensitive solution of iron and platinum salts is applied to paper, contact-printed in daylight for a faint image, then developed out in potassium oxalate. Platinum prints show an extended tonal range, a neutral grey or brown image colour, and a matt finish on plain uncoated paper.

BUYERS' TIP

It is advisable to buy photographs authorized by the artist or his/her estate. These will be stamped or signed.

BUYING GUIDELINES

Focus It is a good idea to specialize in a particular subject – the buildings of Rome or botanical studies made 150 years ago, for example. Successful part-time dealer Patrick Donovan concentrates on French 19th-century erotic art. He finds photos in flea markets in Paris, brings them back to London, hires an exhibition space, and sells at a good profit to collectors.

Where to look The attics of Europe and America are probably still full of boxes of old photographs from yesteryear. There are bargains to be had in most European capitals, especially Paris. This is a particularly good place to look because during the 19th century the French were fascinated by the power of the camera, so correspondingly there is an abundance of images around. It is perfectly possible to pick up old photographs in flea markets for just a few euros. Since the denationalization of the auction houses in Paris (see p.14), the turnover of art, particularly photographs, has been much higher. Photographs are likely to turn up at auction about every six weeks, but the content is less refined than in London and New York auctions, which are held only a couple of times a year. In Paris you might find a photographer on the level of de Prangey, but you will also find very inferior work in abundance.

In New York there are ten times as many buyers as in London, even though the populations of both cities are roughly the same. So buy in Europe and sell in New York – although be aware that tastes are slightly different. An American collector will pay good money for a recognizable image of Europe, but will pay top dollar for an image of vanished America – particularly the Wild West.

Cowboy art Images of Cowboys and Indians in the 1870s and 1880s are particularly sought after as, taken before the age of film, they are one of the few records of a lost way of life. An original photogravure by Edward Curtis, who travelled with cowboys, now sells in a gallery for around $3,200 (£1,800), while a modern silver-gelatin print of his work costs around $320 (£180). Be aware that a modern example will never be as collectable as the photogravure.

Limited editions Today, most professional photographers publish limited editions of their work. They start at the same price, but as the edition runs out prices rise.

The "right kind" of photographer The definition of a photographer has changed. There are those who take pictures primarily for business – magazines, advertising brochures, or commissioned portraits – and there are others who would be described as artists rather than photographers. They choose their own subjects and show in galleries and make very few authenticated prints. Famous examples include William Wegman, Nan Goldin, William Eggleston, and Sam Taylor Wood. At the moment they fetch very high prices and are backed by galleries. An artist who works in the photographic medium with gallery support will always be more valuable than a photographer working for magazines, for example, even though the latter may be very successful and respected.

POSTERS

Rather than being a medium in itself, a poster is an important example of the use of the printing medium. Posters became an effective form of mass communication in the latter half of the 19th century. Colour pages in books and large sheets of printed paper, advertising everything from medicines to theatres, were made possible by the speed at which a lithograph (see Printing Terms Explained, pp.61–3) could be printed – 10,000 sheets an hour was achieved in 1848.

The founding father of poster art was French-born Jules Cheret, who set up his own printing press in the late 1860s with new British machinery. He combined high-quality design with excellent production quality, and his posters advertising the Théâtre de L'Opéra and the opening of the Moulin Rouge are icons of the modern age. His influence on Paris and Parisians was all-pervasive, his dancing girls posters adorning the newly built boulevards of Paris. Even the painter Seurat acknowledged his influence, and without Cheret there would have been no poster art by Alfred Mucha (who immortalized the actress Sarah Bernhardt), Toulouse Lautrec, or Théophile Steinlen (both of whom tinged their work with social comment).

France will always be known as the world centre of poster art, thanks to the Art Nouveau designs of Cheret and his followers and Art Deco posters advertising cigarettes and travel. French artists seem to have achieved a fluidity of style, sharpness, and a simplicity of colour that is unrivalled.

The British poster industry for the most part boasts less flowing graphics, but posters were used extensively by railway companies and seaside towns to encourage tourists. These posters were not produced by artists of the magnitude of Cheret and Lautrec and consequently are less expensive. However, anything by Frank Newbould from the 1920s is worth collecting. Original posters put out by the Government during the world wars, bearing slogans such as "Careless Talk Costs Lives" and other stern messages now also have a value.

HOW POSTERS CAN INCREASE THE PRICE OF PAINTINGS

Of course Dalí, Toulouse Lautrec, and Van Gogh were valuable long before posters were made of their work, but there is no doubt that posters of Jack Vettriano's work have helped to add value to it. Jack Vettriano is not represented in any British gallery; indeed art experts regard his starkly lit paintings, which have been described as a mixture of Edward Hopper and Art Deco posters, with contempt. Despite this, Scottish-born Vettriano is one of the entertainment industry's favourite artists, collected by Jack Nicholson, Tim Rice, and Robbie Coltrane, and his posters out-sell those of Van Gogh, Monet, and Dalí. The ubiquity of his work in the form of posters, which themselves may have no intrinsic value, was probably the major factor in the phenomenal increase in the price of his original paintings in recent years. In 2004 one of his best-known images sold for £744,800 ($1,340,600), which represented a price increase of 2,300 per cent in just six years.

The Communist government of Russia used posters extensively. The best artists, working from the Revolution and through the 1920s, were less influenced by the Art Nouveau style of the French and more by Cubism and the 1920s Bauhaus architecture and furniture school, based in Germany. This style is characterized by the glorification of the machine and the juxtaposition of hard lines and shapes, often in black and red, by artists such as El Lissitzky and Klutsis.

Poster plates produced between 1860 and 1890 were made of limestone. By the turn of the 20th century posters started to be printed from metal plates (lithographs), and most recently, in the modern age, they are digitally printed using computers. With the advent of television, less importance and less excellent creative input were channelled into poster communication, as advertisers now wanted a piece of the new electronic medium. During the 1970s and 1980s the need to hire good artists to draw posters declined dramatically, as the more impersonal computer took over.

Posters dating from 1860 to 1940 are known as vintage posters. Most have a value in excess of £300 ($540), and they are offered for sale at auction houses and galleries throughout the world. Collectors have recently woken up to the artistic merit and affordable starting price for high-quality poster work, so there are now more poster collectors chasing after a finite market.

> **BUYERS' TIP**
> Posters printed before the advent of photographic and computer-based techniques are the most valuable.

BUYING GUIDELINES

Condition As with any form of art, condition is important. However, because posters were printed on low-quality paper and not stored with care like oil paintings, there are bound to be tears. Collectors accept this and will not refuse to pay good money for a poster because of a tiny nick in the corner.

Original prints Posters are valued according to the plate from which they were taken. A poster from original plates would have been overseen by the artist, art director, or photographer on the advertising campaign. A good-quality Toulouse Lautrec reproduction printed in the 1940s has only a decorative value. The original lithograph from limestone is what everyone wants.

Original posters from the late 19th and early and mid-20th centuries are fetching high prices today. Posters have always been essentially disposable, so early ones have a rarity value. Originally posters were printed from an artist's sketch, but in most cases these were not kept, as they were not considered important. Therefore posters from the original plates are the nearest we can get to the artist's original work.

It is very difficult for amateurs to tell the difference between originals and later copies. Christie's vintage poster expert Nicolette Tomkinson says you can only really tell by putting a later copy alongside the original.

Quality Posters were devised not for lengthy perusal but for immediate impact, so at a glance the best posters are witty, simple, and well laid out. In the case of travel or advertising posters, the subject portrayed should have a glamorous appeal. For example, the work of early 20th-century Italian Leonetto Cappiello is a favourite among poster collectors in the United States for its wit. His posters are subtle in that they do not always depict the product, but rather are clever and amusing images associated with what he is trying to sell.

Age versus theme The age of a poster is not so important, because most poster collectors buy according to theme. Art Deco travel posters are particularly popular, as we associate this style with luxury and glamour.

Film posters The area of film posters is not a dealer-led market. It is very difficult, if not impossible, to predict good investments. Film posters tend to be more photographic, and less sellable on the basis of who they are by. Image is what sells a film poster, and they can be divided into two areas: genre posters (horror, Western, the films of Alfred Hitchcock) and personality (Clint Eastwood, Ava Gardner, Elvis Presley). In the genre category, early horror posters are popular at the

RISING PRICES

Prices have been rising steadily over the last few decades. A Toulouse Lautrec poster printed from an original plate could be bought for $50 (£18) in the1950s, but today you would not get much change from $400,000 (£220,000) for one of his best. The work of Jules Cheret, which, according to Jack Rennert, President of Posters Please and Poster Auctions International Inc. in New York, shows irrepressible vitality and soaring beauty in everything he drew, for cigarette and brandy companies as well as many other businesses, can be had for much less. His prices are rising too, though. In 1990 a work by Cheret fetched an average of $2,000 (£1,250); today the same poster would fetch around $8,000 (£4,500).

moment. The film poster market is strongly dictated by personal taste and prices can fluctuate as a result. Specialist Sarah Hodgson has noticed, however, that, as with photography, certain celebrities are always more popular: eternal icons such as Audrey Hepburn, Steve McQueen, and Sean Connery as James Bond. Film posters included in auctions or sold in galleries have to have been printed at the time of a film's release, although Sarah Hodgson cites a few exceptions, such as the re-release poster of the Paul Newman film *The Hustler*. This is more popular than the one from the original release, as the re-release version depicts the famous pool scene.

Psychedelic posters An emerging market, fuelled by nostalgic baby boomers – children of the 1960s and 70s – and their children, who love Jimi Hendrix and other music from his era, is in what are now known as psychedelic posters. These brightly coloured posters were produced to promote concerts and record releases. As yet they do not fetch very much money, but good examples are being included in auction house sales.

Soviet posters Propaganda posters from the Soviet era currently do not have a strong value in the West. The Russians themselves are only just coming to terms with the Stalinist era and are not as yet great buyers. As the free market economy grows in the former USSR, however, posters from the Revolution through to the 1930s are starting to change hands for increasing sums. There is a market in Germany for the graphic abstract constructivist work of El Lissitksy, G. Klutsis, and Vladimir Lebedev, printed during the 1920s. The posters Stalin ordered in the following decade were less abstract and more of smiling and happy farm and factory workers. These do not have the same artistic merit as the Constructivist posters and are not so desirable today.

Buying on the Internet There are countless companies on the Internet selling posters, most of which have no resale value. It is not a good idea to buy a vintage poster off the Internet unless an expert from a company recommends it to you. An auction house or specialist dealer is a good place to buy posters because a professional has estimated their value in a historical context. They also sell original posters with provenance: auction houses do not sell valueless decorative posters.

DIGITAL & MULTIMEDIA ART

In general terms, the word "multimedia" might refer to a mixture of any of the media we have previously discussed. In a more specific context, however, text, audio, graphics, animation, video, and "interactive" elements are the more typical components. Even more specifically, the term is often used to refer to a combination of digital or computer-based media, including LCD lighting, lasers, or digital images printed onto paper or board or displayed on a screen for instance, with sensors and mechanics often used in order to make pieces move or react to stimuli. The sophistication of the personal computer today now allows manipulation to an extent that was not available to artists even just a decade ago, and many young artists are using digital technology to excellent effect – the best of their work will become highly collectable in the future.

Computers have been around for over 50 years; originally it was the military that employed the gigantic ancestor of the personal computer. As with video, artists really started to use the medium in the 1960s in the United States. Technicians such as Michael A. Noll, a researcher at the Bell Laboratories in New Jersey, created some of the earliest computer images, which he displayed at an exhibition of computer-generated pictures at the Howard Wise Gallery in New York in 1965. Around this time, John Whitney used a 12-foot high machine that pasted together photographs, creating a single image from them. Other artists fed punched cards into computers to create works of art. This was nearly 30 years before computer-art software such as Photoshop became universally available.

The medium is certainly diverse – for example, 34-year-old

Chris Finley makes use of all sorts of material in his art. Having created a colourful image on his computer by rotating and copying pictorial elements within a design program, he then copies the digital images onto canvas with paint, mixing the colours to correspond to the digital palette. Joseph Nechvatal, 20 years his senior, did not grow up with computer-aided methods of working but is still fascinated by this new medium. He creates what art expert and author Christiane Paul calls "computer-robotic assisted paintings". Apart from his initial artistic composition or manipulation of an image, his work is created totally by machine: he composes a painting on screen and then introduces a virus-like program to transform his work. The result is then transferred, via the Internet, to a remote computer attached to a paint robot "who" then executes the painting. Nechvatal is not involved in applying the paint at all.

Digital artists often reflect the times in which we live – that is, the relation between human and machine. There are certain words used to explain this (see "Explanation of Terms" below). In *Galapagos*, a digital work created by Karl Sims, abstract computer-generated organisms are displayed on twelve screens forming an arc, and viewers choose which life form they prefer by stepping on a sensor in front of the screen.

EXPLANATION OF TERMS
Augmented reality Computer-enhanced physical reality.
Autonomous characters Computer-controlled characters "who" are able to act "freely", aping animal or human characteristics.
Cyberspace A term coined by William Gibson in his novel *Necromancer* to describe a totally computer-generated world.
Hypermedia An extension of mixed media. Artists can use text, audio, film, and anything from the Internet to create a work of art.
Telerobotics Pictures can be painted "telerobotically" by a robot via a computer.

VIDEO ART

Video is a universal medium through which all artists, from Argentina to China, can express themselves, and many increasingly do. When the American Bill Viola showed his works on video, the British media gave him a huge amount of coverage. Video is an easy medium to use, but the art comes when the person operating the camera employs his creative perception and extracts an emotional reaction from the viewer in response to what they see.

Video art can be interactive, as when people are photographed or filmed reacting to a situation or an image, but this has to be manipulated with care by the artist. One of the first installations of video art was in 1969, when Americans Frank Gillette and Ira Schneider featured nine video monitors, four of which showed pre-taped material (some taken from television shows) and five of which played live and delayed images of viewers as they entered the gallery. Here the artists manipulated time to interesting effect.

The great advantage that video art has over other forms of art is its ability to tell a story through a moving image. The disadvantage is that many pieces are made for gallery shows and do not enter the commercial domain. It is not easy to display three video monitors in the average home. However, with prices of flat screen monitors falling and technology becoming more and more sophisticated, it is now possible to encase moving images in a flat plasma screen to hang on the wall – and art dealers do indeed sell limited-edition video art.

BUYERS' TIP
Work by well-respected digital artists can be bought for as little as £500 ($900).

ARTISTS USING WORDS

Before the 20th century a jumble of words on a canvas or in lights would not have been considered art. Now these works come under the broad umbrella of Conceptual art (*see* Movements, Schools, & Styles, p.175), and fine examples are to be found in the best museums in the world. Artists well known for their use of words during the 1960s and 1970s are Ed Ruscha, Robert Barry, and Joseph Kosuth. They sought to extend the Dadaist view of the definition of art. "I use words because they speak to the viewer. Words come from us. We can relate to them. They bridge the gap between the viewer and the piece," remarked Robert Barry in 1983.

These artists also felt a strong desire to theorize about the meaning of art. Robert Baldessari produced an oil on canvas that was entirely text-based, called *What This Painting Aims to Do*. This art gathered momentum and was a very popular form of artistic expression during the 1980s and 1990s in Britain as well as in the United States. Successful and highly acclaimed practitioners were the American Hamish Fulton, Irish artist Kathy Prendergast, and American-English artist Susan Hiller.

A good deal of text-based art is made specially for museums and public places and is not for resale – with the exception of that of Ed Ruscha, which starts at $50,000 (£27,500) for a drawing and reaches up to $1million (£550,000) for other media. However, some of Robert Barry's good work can be had for $6,000 (£3,300) and Joseph Kosuth's for $15,000 (£8,300). Similarly, despite Fulton, Prendergast, and Hiller being featured in museums and books about art, much of their work is available from $1,000 to $5,000 (£550 to £2,700).

Words can also be used alongside images. In 1993, British-born Gillian Wearing executed a series of photographs of people holding placards, entitled *Signs That Say What You Want Them To Say and Not Signs That Say What Someone Else Wants You To Say*. Limited editions of these are offered for sale for $15,000 (£8,300).

BUYING GUIDELINES

Speculate Video and digital art are just getting into their stride. Observe, learn, and get in early. As technology gets faster and cheaper and picture quality and the capacity to manipulate images improve, young artists will make very interesting work.

Authenticity Always buy video art from a reputable dealer. Insist on authentic documentation to prove its merit and ensure that you are buying a limited edition. At present there is no secondary market, such as auctions, for video art.

Quality When investing in video art, apply the same judgments as you would for paintings or any other art works. Video is just another medium, and should stand up to the same scrutiny. However advanced the technology gets, video art is only good if the imagery and creativity involved are good.

The London scene The Haunch of Venison gallery in London is one of the leaders in the video art field and represents the American artist Bill Viola. His work is expensive: he will create a limited edition of six films set in a wall-mounted black monitor for $50,000 (£27,500) each. But work by less well-known yet still well-respected video artists at this gallery can be bought for around £1,800 ($3,200).

Prices According to Graham Southern, of the Haunch of Venison gallery, video art prices can spiral if production costs are high. He also acknowledges that the technology is getting more advanced and, in some cases, cheaper all the time, so you are getting more for your money in terms of technique.

Forgery Graham Southern also reckons that video art is much harder to forge than any other medium because, along with your DVD and monitor, you get authentication documentation signed by the artist that you need to show if you come to sell. A copy will usually also be lodged at the gallery.

Text-based art There is no unifying theme running through text-based art. The piece can be a single word, a random arrangement of phrases, a philosophical thought, or a political sentiment, so buy what appeals to you.

Museum standard Try and buy text pieces by artists whose work has also been bought by a major museum. As mentioned, much text-based work was created for museum installations.

SCULPTURE

Humans have carved solid material from time immemorial. Ancient civilizations would place tiny effigies in burial chambers to ward off spirits, or make woodcarvings to encourage the deities to send down rain. The Greeks and Romans carved celebrated images of their gods.

In the West today, most of those who commission or collect sculpture do so for more secular reasons – we do not necessarily worship (in a spiritual sense) at the feet of Shiva or Apollo. Nor would we put a carving by our bed to help us conceive a baby: we turn to science for that. The pleasure a 21st-century person derives from sculpture is more to do with how it makes us feel inside. Instead of spiritual comfort or guidance, we are more likely to seek aesthetically pleasing objects.

Good sculpture appeals not only to the eyes, but to the sense of touch as well.

This book cannot begin to cover in any depth the work of sculptors over the millennia, so it will concentrate on what appeals to modern collectors. A perennially popular field of sculpture for collectors, for instance, is cast bronzes of animals (known as "Animalia"), with leopards and other big cats leading the field, followed by dogs and horses.

As the human race became more "civilized" and less close to nature, people became shocked and fascinated by anything of a particularly graphic nature. Even today, to some Western eyes an African carving of an erect penis or a woman with huge breasts might seem primitive or even pornographic. In 19th-century France there were angry letters to the newspapers because the casts by Antoine-Louis Barye, depicting a lion killing a hare for example, broke with the classical tradition by being so convincingly and frighteningly natural. The Victorians professed to be shocked at the sight of the naked body, yet they were keen collectors and buyers of nude sculptures because they considered them to be "high art" from, or inspired by, the classical era. Today we claim not to be so easily shocked, yet Jake and Dinos Chapman certainly try. These English brothers produce dolls with penises sticking out of their heads. Their macabre appearance might not be to all tastes, but they feature in museum and exclusive collections.

Tribal art, on the other hand, ceased to be so shocking some time ago. Needless to say, in our more liberated era sexualized sculpture in the form of bronze or wood African fertility symbols, often with exaggerated genitalia, is now very collectable. Work from the Dogon people of Mali and the Yoruba tribe of Nigeria is especially appreciated by Western collectors, and many tribal pieces tie in well with contemporary paintings. Indeed, it is well known that the early French Impressionists were fascinated by tribal art. African influences can also be seen in the work of Picasso.

READY-MADE, FOUND OBJECTS, & CONSTRUCTIVISM

People were also shocked by what became known as ready-made sculpture, where artists turned found objects into sculpture, and the disgusted establishment figures shouted "This is not art!" The birth of this form of sculpture, which also comes under the banner of Conceptual art (see Movements, Schools, & Styles, p.175), is generally credited to Marcel Duchamp, who famously signed and displayed a urinal in 1917. Duchamp and his followers maintained that sculpture no longer needed to be fashioned from bronze or stone, but could be assembled from everyday objects. Braque and Picasso also used found materials, gluing and welding pre-formed pieces together. They believed that this "Assemblage art", as it was then known, was the new and exciting way forward, but it did not attract many followers in the United States and Britain until the 1950s.

It was Russian artists who took up the ready-made baton, but there Assemblage art extended into a movement known as Russian Constructivism. These sculptures were likewise made from pieces of metal, glass, wood, cardboard, or plastic, but they sought to emphasize space rather than mass. Vladimir Tatlin had seen Picasso's assemblages or collages in 1913, before returning to Russia to make, in the opinion of art observers, the first abstract sculptures.

Constructivist sculptures were often prototypes and ideas for factories and public buildings, and even Alexander Rodchenko's hanging constructions feel as if they are molecules explained and have some educational use. This scientific rationality in art appealed to the Soviet government, although when Stalin came to power the Constructivists split into two factions. One made utilitarian and didactic designs for the masses, and the other preferred to make more introspective pieces. The latter group were considered too decadent and felt obliged to flee to the West (*see* Affordable Fields to Consider Now, p.103).

As the 20th century progressed, more materials became available for sculptors to work with. Fluorescent lighting tubes, all kinds of plastic, and aluminium were now at their disposal.

Minimalist was a name given to a group of artists and sculptors working in the United States in the 1960s: Carl Andre, Dan Flavin, Donald Judd, Sol Le Witt, and Robert Morris. They disliked the term Minimalist, but their work has in common the use of ready-made materials, which are often formed into cubes and rectangles. They did not carve out of stone and there were no soft lines in their work. Despite public outrage in some quarters

SCULPTURE TERMS EXPLAINED

Abozzo This term refers to the rough shaping of a piece of stone before it is finely carved.

Alabaster A soft translucent stone that can be found in pink, pure white, and pale blue-grey, sometimes heavily veined. It is easy to carve and can be given a highly polished finish.

Basalt This is dark in colour and, like granite, is extremely hard and requires special tools to carve it. It is attractive to sculptors because it can be highly polished. Some types have a naturally glassy texture.

Base Sculpture is often displayed on a base or a plinth.

Bronze A very popular material for cast sculpture. It is an alloy of copper and tin and sometimes a small amount of another metal, such as zinc or lead. Sculptors like it because it is strong, with great tensile strength, and reproduces fine detail well. There is no precise formula for bronze, and its colour depends on the proportions of the different metals used. Copper is, however, the main ingredient.

Cast A three-dimensional sculpture that is produced in a mould. Moulds are now often made of silicone rubber because of its flexible properties.

Installation An installation is a collection of objects that together make an artistic statement; this may include sculpture or objects that may feasibly be seen as sculpture. These objects could be chairs, ropes, a film showing on a screen – anything really.

Maquette A small preparatory sculpture for a larger work, traditionally made in clay and sometimes carved. When dealers cannot exhibit huge sculptures in their galleries, they ask the sculptor to make a maquette to show prospective buyers. Maquettes have value but less than the original sculpture, and there may be many maquettes for one work.

Multiple A multiple is a three-dimensional artwork produced in quantities. The work of Conceptual and Minimalist sculptors is sometimes produced in multiples, albeit not large in number.

(*see* chapter two, What is Art?, p.24) Minimalism is going from strength to strength, with exhibitions of the masters' work proving very popular. Donald Judd is certainly a blue-chip artist, his work now joining the league of great sculptors who, if you had the money, would certainly make a sound investment.

The term "found object" can also refer to objects from nature, as opposed to the manufactured kind used by Minimalists. Britain has a good stable of living artists working in stones and petrified bodies or body parts. For example, a Minimalist might use a box as a sculpture, but Damien Hirst puts a preserved shark inside it. He and other sculptor-artists emerging in London since the 1980s have become more interested in the visceral: elephant dung in Chris Ofili's case and his own dried blood in Mark Quinn's. Others like uncarved stone and wood in an outside setting, often on a monumental scale – Richard Long and Andy Goldsworthy being two of the most famous.

ANCIENT SCULPTURE

It is possible to form a collection of beautiful pieces of ancient art or antiquities from both the West and the East. Look back in time: sculpture lasts well and you can still buy pieces from ancient Greece and Rome and from Islamic civilizations made 1,000 years ago. You would have thought that these ancient artifacts, many of which could easily be in a museum, would be prohibitively expensive, but this is very often not the case. In 18th-century Britain, for example, gentlemen would travel through Europe on a Grand Tour of ancient sites and bring home small artifacts. Some of these pieces, hidden away in stately home cupboards for over 200 years, are now coming up for sale. For example, a Roman head and torso of Venus from the 1st century AD, 28cm (11in) high, can be bought for around $2,000 (£1,100). An Etruscan figure of a woman from the 6th century BC can be bought for around $5,000 (£2,700), two tiny Greek terracotta heads from the 5th century BC for $3,000 (£1,600), or a South Arabian calcite head from the 1st century BC for $7,000 (£3,800) – bargains compared with 20th-century sculptures by Rembrandt Bugatti, Henry Moore, or Richard Long for instance.

Affordable antiquities Size matters – large pieces are very expensive, while small pieces often get overlooked, even though they may still be exquisite and interesting articles, and prices can be very reasonable. Beware of the risk of illegal importation (see p.157).

Provenance It is vital that any antiquities you buy come with appropriate provenance to prove their authenticity. Buy only from a respected dealer or from a collection formed by experts in the 18th or 19th century.

Classical replicas Victorian and Georgian replicas of classical busts are currently a bargain, but seek out the best examples. There are countless poorly made plaster casts and they are to be avoided. They are cheap, but there is a reason for this.

Tribal art It is very hard to date African tribal art because tribespeople have been making work in the same manner for centuries. For this reason auction houses do not attempt to date pieces such as this in their catalogues.

Although very fine Dogon and Yoruba pieces sell for many thousands, a huge number of masks, shields, and hand-carved eating dishes sell for just a few hundred pounds. It is a good idea to buy from a private collection formed in the United States or Europe. Auctioneers will always head the sale "Property from the Estate of William Kohler" (or whoever). These pieces are more likely to be genuine and carved for devotion, fighting, or eating rather than for tourists. Tribal pieces are now knocked out for the tourist trade, but many are very shoddily worked.

Abstract versus figurative sculpture Abstract work is now part of the mainstream canon, although watch out for a return to more figurative forms – the well-known British abstract sculptor Sir Anthony Caro recently created figures sitting at a table. Investing in more figurative sculpture by a well-respected artist may be a wise move.

BUYING GUIDELINES

Price range Sculptures by Renaissance masters and big pieces from ancient civilizations are priceless, and affordable only by large organizations. Donald Judd, one of the most influential figures of the post-war period, is far beyond the average art budget, along with superstars such as Rodin, Brancusi, Canova, and the big British names of the 20th century, such as Moore and Hepworth. But as sculpture has always been perceived as the poor relation of painting, with the exception of these very famous names, the most valuable sculpture is either very old or

> **BUYERS' TIP**
> With so much ancient art forgery around, insist on getting all the proper provenance and paperwork for anything you buy.

very new, and prices are generally lower than for paintings. However, with Conceptual and Minimalist pieces now being so fashionable and collectable, things are beginning to change.

Conceptual sculpture Of course some Conceptual art, such as men walking round with slogans on their backs, has no commercial value, but solid and tangible pieces are very saleable, very popular, and have the fastest investment potential of all styles of art. Conceptual sculpture is highly desirable to wealthy collectors today. The work of Sol Le Witt or Donald Judd can fetch six figures in dollars, pounds, and euros. Dan Flavin's neon light sculptures go for mid-five-figure sums in US dollars, as do Carl Andre's wood and brick pieces. Robert Morris pieces have also been selling over their auction estimates (low five figures in US dollars) in the last few years.

The galleries in London's East End are where you will find interesting Conceptual art and ready-made sculptures. Indeed, some investors have made a killing in the last few years. In 1997 a good piece using glass and neon lights by British duo Tim Noble and Sue Webster was sold by their dealers, Modern Art Inc, for around £5,000 ($8,000). Recently another good piece by them was sold at auction for nearly £100,000 ($180,000). They have become hot property, with museum exhibitions devoted to them.

Conceptual quality Because Conceptual and Minimalist art are so glamorous in the eyes of collectors and art school graduates, there are many poor imitations of the masters. So it is worth buying a good name to secure lasting value, such as an artist with international exhibition status or one who has been offered for sale in a reputable gallery (such as Leo Castelli in New York, Galerie Yvon Lambert in Paris, or Gagosian, who have galleries in London, New York, and Beverly Hills – *see* Useful Contacts,

Events, & Reference, pp.89–90). These galleries' top artists are very expensive, so look for new talent they are bringing on.

However, in the case of Minimalist and Conceptual sculpture, it is better to buy a lesser work by a great artist than a great work by a lesser artist. This maxim does not apply to all fields of art, but it is appropriate in this case. Many of these sculptors made sketches and drawings – Sol Le Witt and Donald Judd's pencil and pen-and-ink drawings can be had for around $5,000 (£2,700), and Nic Fiddian Green (*see* below) sells beautiful chalk drawings of his horse-head sculptures that start at around £1,000 ($1,800). Begin with a drawing and then move on to a small sculpture.

Animal sculpture Animalia is a crowded market within the US and the UK; there are many artists working in the field, so make sure you buy a good piece by a well-regarded artist. Among the most famous and sought-after work is that by the sculptor Rembrandt Bugatti, who cast bronzes in the Art Deco style. One of his 70cm (28in) cats could fetch up to £1 million ($1.8 million), but an eagle by him could possibly be had for £12,000 ($21,500). In the case of Bugatti, buy anything by him if it can be authenticated – he lived only to the age of 32.

Nic Fiddian Green, who is one of Britain's most promising contemporary animal sculptors, casts horses in bronze. To commission a large piece for a public display will cost £100,000 ($180,000), a horse for your garden around £20,000 ($36,000).

Animalia can be found in Paris flea markets in particular, because much was made in France at bargain prices. You might find a piece for a few euros that could be worth considerably more. But fakes and copies beyond the limited editions commissioned by the galleries abound, and unless you are an expert it is very difficult to tell the difference. Check if the piece has a recognizable stamp from a foundry that is authorized by the sculptor.

Editions Galleries usually recommend casting nine editions, and so these are usually the most valuable. Inevitably more get made (indeed Barye decided to sell directly to the public, turning out many small animals). Dan Flavin, among others, produced many of his neon sculptures in editions of five. Get a certificate of authenticity – in this case signed by him.

LABELS AND TITLES CAN BE CONFUSING

Tate Britain has become concerned that labels and descriptions of Conceptual art and sculpture have become too pretentious and incomprehensible – one esoteric caption under a Richard Long arrangement of slate pieces in a circle reads: "The contrast between the geometry of the circle and the irregular contours of the material objects in this piece suggests the presence of man in the landscape… The circular arrangement is an imposed order on the flatness of each piece, which is characteristic of slate, representing a natural order." Is it? So they have invited members of the public to offer their own descriptions.

A recent television programme showed the reluctance of contemporary British sculptors to talk about their work because so much artwork is beyond description. However, a full and detailed description does help to sell a piece. An interesting recent Conceptual piece that was sold at Christie's and had formerly been on display was a stuffed horse hanging from a hoist by Italian artist Cattelan. The title, *The Ballad of Trotsky*, might not immediately spring to mind on looking at a dead horse, so we will have to let the Christie's catalogue entry explain. "*The Ballad of Trotsky* is a powerfully persuasive work about the tragedy of being unable to act or effect change. In this work Italian Maurizio Cattelan presents the shock of a startling single image isolated against a large and open space. A horse, that perennial symbol of strength and harnessed power, has been harnessed in space in such a way as to become useless, like the tragic example of the idealist leader of the Russsian Revolution, Leon Trotsky." The piece sold at Christie's in London in 2001 for £619,000 ($930,000). It then came up for sale in 2004 at Sotheby's in New York with an estimate of $600,000 to $800,000 and sold for $2 million (£1.3 million).

BUYERS' TIP

The most saleable sculptured animals are big cats, any African animal, and horses.

USEFUL CONTACTS, EVENTS, & REFERENCE

PAINTING AND GENERAL

The Armory Show This New York event is the leading art fair in the United States and shows many painters including contemporary New York artists. Visit www.thearmoryshow.com or call +1 212 645 6440.

Artists and Illustrators This magazine claims to be the UK's best-selling art magazine. Its approach is populist and practical, mixing profiles on affordable artists and those who are going up in price with practical tips for artists, which might aid your understanding of art. Published monthly. Visit www.aimag.co.uk or call Quarto publishing on +44 (0)20 7700 8500 for details.

Art on Paper Fair This fair is held in London in February. Prices start at £50 ($90), and Japanese, Chinese, and British contemporary art on paper, as well as 19th-century watercolours, are on show. Visit www.artonpaper.co.uk.

Auctions Auctions of drawings and watercolours are frequently held by all the major auction houses, both in Europe and the United States (*see* Directory, p.183). Christie's South Kensington, London, has a weekly sale of paintings. You can sometimes find interesting work there. Visit www.christies.com or call +44 (0)20 7930 6074.

Gagosian This gallery has branches in London, New York, and Beverly Hills, and also publishes books on modern artists and sculptors. Visit www.gagosian.com or call London on +44 (0)207 841 9960 or New York on +1 212 741 1111.

Haunch of Venison This London gallery shows the most fashionable artists, including figurative work. Visit www.haunchofvenison.com or call +44 (0)20 7495 5050.

Inspired Art Fair For new and exciting artworks it is worth visiting this fair, in November. Based in London's East End, the artists' quarter of the city, the event is strictly vetted to keep the standard high, with many works for sale under £2,500 ($4,500). Call +44 (0)208 374 7318 or visit www.inspiredartfair.com for further details.

Leo Castelli This New York gallery is one of the most established contemporary art galleries in North America, and has shown some of the biggest names in the modern art world. Visit www.leocastelligallery.com or call +1 212 249 4470.

Lisson Gallery Based in London, this gallery represents Tony Cragg, Anish Kapoor, and other great sculptors and artists. Visit www.lisson.co.uk or call +44 (0)207 724 2739.

London Art Fair Every January, Britain's longest-running art fair has a good selection of paintings from the present back to the beginning of the 20th century. Visit www.londonartfair.co.uk or call +44 (0)20 7359 3535.

Tate Gallery To check out artists, visit www.tate.org.uk and see their database of over 65,000 paintings and sculpture from their four galleries in Britain, thousands of which are illustrated.

Victoria and Albert Museum This London museum holds an archive of over 750,000 prints, drawings, paintings, and photographs, which are worth making a trip to see even though you won't be able to buy them. Make an appointment by calling +44 (0)207 492 2563, or view an increasing number online by accessing the museum's website at www.vam.ac.uk.

Yvon Lambert This leading contemporary art gallery in Paris and New York shows artists working in all media. Visit www.yvon-lambert.com or call Paris on +33 (0)1 42 71 09 33 or New York on +1 212 242 3611.

DRAWINGS AND SKETCHES

The Master Drawings in London Week This takes place every year for a week in July, when West End galleries put on special exhibitions of old and new master drawings. For further information visit www.masterdrawingsinlondon.co.uk or call +44 (0)207 439 2882.

Watercolours and Drawings Fair Held every February in London, this fair has good coverage of the 20th century. Visit www.watercoloursfair.com for more details or call +44 (0) 7000 785 613.

ASIAN AND TRIBAL ART

Asian and Tribal Art Show Los Angeles hosts this fair in October every year. Visit www.caskeylees.com or call +1 310 455 2886.

Asian Art Fair For those wanting to see all types of Asian art, paintings, drawings, prints, and sculpture, a visit to the Asian Art Fair in London in November is well worthwhile. Visit www.asianartinlondon.com or call +44 (0)207 499 2215.

Asian Art News A good Far Eastern and international art resource, published in Hong Kong but distributed in Europe and North America. Call them in Hong Kong on +852 2522 3443 or visit the website, www.asianartnews.com.

Christie's The London and New York offices of the auction house hold regular Tribal Art sales. Visit www.christies.com or call South Kensington on +44 (0)20 7930 6074 and New York on +1 212 636 2000 for further information.

The International Asian Art Fair Held in New York every March, this brings together dealers in everything Eastern – bronzes, pictures, textiles, etc. Organized by the London-based Haughton International Fairs. Visit www.haughton.com or call + 44 (0)20 7734 5491.

COWBOY AND AMERICAN ART

Altermann Galleries and Collectors Fair Cowboy and Wild West art can be seen at this fair in Dallas, Texas. Call +1 214 871 3055 for more information.

National Cowboy & Western Heritage Museum Based in Oklahoma City. Visit www.nationalcowboymuseum.org or call +1 405 478 2250.

Who's Who in American Art A book of listings that includes artists and others working in the art field (museum personnel, librarians, educators, critics, dealers, etc.). Covers living persons only in the United States, Canada, and Mexico. (Marquis Who's Who, New Providence, 2005).

Who Was Who in American Art 1564–1975 This three-volume tome covers 400 years of art in America, including illustrations of signatures where relevant (Peter H. Falk (Editor), Madison CT, Sound View Press, 1999).

PORTRAITS

Historical Portraits Ltd A specialist in British and American portraiture, working closely with national museums and institutions. Able to trace family portraits. Visit www.historicalportraits.com or 31 Dover Street, London W1S 4ND, or call +44 (0)207 499 6818.

National Portrait Gallery This London gallery's collection includes over 300,000 works, 60,574 of which are listed online, 40,288 of them illustrated, and the database is constantly being expanded. Visit www.npg.org.uk.

PRINTS

International Fine Print Dealers Association The IFPDA is a non-profit organization based in New York dedicated to ensuring the highest ethical standards among print dealers. The association has a list of members who meet its exacting standards, publishes a newsletter, and organizes talks and lectures to do with prints. It also recommends print fairs at which you can buy everything from Old Masters to Modern, American, European, and Japanese prints. The fairs are held in New York at the beginning of November in conjunction with the city's Print Week, and in Seattle, San Francisco, and Los Angeles every January. Call +1 212 674 6095 or visit the website www.printdealers.com for further details.

London Original Print Fair Established in 1985, this fair takes place annually at the Royal Academy of Arts in London. Prints on display range from early examples of printmaking, such as the 15th-century engravings and woodcuts of Dürer, to the most recent work of contemporary printmakers, such as David Hockney and Damien Hirst. Visit www.londonprintfair.com or call +44 (0)207 439 2000 for details.

PHOTOGRAPHY

Christie's Christie's South Kensington, London, has well-informed photographic experts and very good twice-yearly sales. Call +44 (0)20 7839 9060. Christie's New York (+1 212 636 2000) and Christie's Los Angeles (+1 310 385 2600) also have sales of good quality photographs – www.christies.com.

Dominic Winter Book Auctions Based in Swindon, UK, this auctioneer has specialist sales of aviation military transport, which include photographs. They also sell cinema archives, including posters and photographs. Call +44 (0)1793 611340 or visit www.dominicwinter.co.uk.

Edwynn Houk Gallery This New York gallery represents a good cross-section of European and American top-ranking photographers. Visit www.houkgallery.com or call + 1 212 750 7070.

Howard Greenberg An important New York photographic dealer. At this gallery you will see the best examples of photojournalism by well-respected photographers. Visit www.howardgreenberg.com or call + 1 212 334 0010.

Hypnos Gallery This Paris dealer always has good examples of 19th-century landscape photographs by recognized masters of the genre. Visit www.hypnos-photo.com (in French) or call +33 1 45 44 99 71.

Michael Hoppen Gallery This London gallery is a good place to see the work of interesting contemporary photographers. Visit www.michaelhoppengallery.com or call +44 (0)20 7352 3649.

National Gallery of Canada This was one of the first museums to collect photographs. These, together with their collection of American, European, and Asian art, can be viewed online – the site even includes some pieces not on view in the galleries at www.national.gallery.ca. Tel: +1 613 990 1985.

Photo London UK "PLUK" was one of the first organizations to mount photography exhibitions in the capital. Held at the Royal Academy every May, it is an exciting show with works at all prices. Visit www.photo-london.com or call +44 (0)20 7839 9300.

Tajan This Paris auction house has twice-yearly sales. You could find a masterpiece here by an as yet unknown French photographer. Visit www.tajan.com or call +33 1 53 30 30 79.

POSTERS

Christie's The South Kensington branch has a number of poster sales every year, including a Ski sale dedicated entirely to winter sports, a vintage poster sale, and a British and Irish Travel sale including posters from seaside towns. They also have film poster and pop memorabilia sales. For further information visit www.christies.com or call +44 (0)207 839 9060.

Deutsches Historisches Museum This Berlin museum has a comprehensive poster collection that can be viewed online at www.dhm.de. Tel: +49 (0)30 20304 0.

International Poster Center and Poster Auctions International Information, exhibitions, and twice-yearly poster auctions at 601 West 26th Street, New York. Visit www.postersplease.com or call + 1 212 787 4000.

The Reel Poster Gallery A specialist in original film posters, whose co-owner Tony Nourmand has written numerous books on the subject. Visit the shop at 72 Westbourne Grove, London, or www.reelposter.com, or call +44 (0)207 727 4488.

VIDEO ART

Chambers Fine Art This gallery in New York is a good place to look for video art. Visit www.chambersfineart.com or call +1 212 414 1169.

Haunch of Venison Bill Viola is among the various contemporary artists represented by this London gallery. *See* p.89 for contact details.

Video Art Festival Locarno This festival in Locarno, Switzerland, has been going for 25 years and is for those seriously interested in collecting video art. Visit the website (in Italian) at www.tinet.ch/videoart or call +41 91 751 22 08.

TEXT-BASED ART

The following galleries represent text-based artists:

Gabrielle Salomon – Art Conseil Based in Paris, visit www.gabriellesalomon.com or call +33 (0)1 45 27 33 40.

Galerie Anselm Dreher Based in Berlin, visit www.galerie-anselm-dreher.com or call +49 (0)30 883 52 49.

Marian Goodman Gallery This New York gallery represents John Badessari and has been instrumental in showing new and interesting international contemporary artists since 1977. They also have a gallery in Paris. Visit www.mariangoodman.com or call New York: +1 212 977 7160 or Paris: +33 1 48 04 70 52.

Tate Modern London's big modern-art gallery contains text-based work by various artists. Visit www.tate.org.uk/modern or call +44 (0)20 7887 8000.

SCULPTURE

Acquavella Gallery Interesting 20th-century sculpture is shown at this New York gallery. Visit www.acquavellagalleries.com or call +1 212 734 6300.

Alchemy of Sculpture This book gives a lot of information on cast and carved sculpture. (Tony Birks, Yeovil, Marston House, 2004.)

Antiquities Dealers Association This London-based organization aims to help collectors enjoy their hobby by promoting the ethical collecting of antiquities. Visit www.the-ada.org or call +44 (0) 207 930 1864.

Brook Green Gardens These gardens are home to the Huntington Sculpture Garden and indoor sculpture galleries, near Myrtle Beach, North Carolina. The collection contains over 900 works for your inspiration, spanning American sculpture from the early 1800s to the present. Visit www.brookgreen.org or call +1 843 235 6000.

Christie's Every December Christie's holds a tribal art sale at their Paris office. Call +33 1 40 76 83 86. Catalogues can be viewed online at www.christies.com.

The Dictionary of Sculptors in Bronze This comprehensive work by James Mackay lists thousands of artists who worked in bronze from the 18th century to 1960. Published in England in 1977, it is still available from the Antique Collectors' Club (Woodbridge). Visit www.antique-acc.com or call +44 (0)1394 389977.

Encyclopedia of Sculpture Edited by Antonia Bostrom, this is a comprehensive three-volume book on sculpture with extensive biographies of sculptors and in-depth explanations of trends, from Renaissance Italy to the present day, and also encompassing sculpture in Africa and Asia. (Fitzroy Dearborn, London and New York, 2002). Visit www.fitzroydearborn.com.

Grizedale Forest Park In the heart of England's Lake District, Richard Long and Andy Goldsworthy, among others, have made site-specific pieces, displayed among the trees. If you are thinking of commissioning a sculpture for your garden this is the place to go to get ideas. Visit Grizedale Arts at www.grizedale.org or call +44 (0)1229 860 291.

The Hannah Peschar Sculpture Garden Hannah and her landscape designer husband Anthony Paul have created an intimate garden of smaller affordable pieces by new talent alongside work by leading British and international artists, at their home in Surrey, England. Most are for sale. Visit www.hannahpescharsculpture.com or call +44 (0)1306 627 269.

The International Asian Art Fair This includes sculpture. *See* "Asian and Tribal Art", p. 91.

London Sculpture Week This takes place every June and comprises an interesting mix of sculpture dealers. Visit www.londonsculptureweek.com or call +44 (0)20 7493 0688.

Maastricht (TEFAF) This fair in Belgium is one of Europe's premier art and antiques fairs, showing top-quality sculpture every March. Visit www.tefaf.com or call +31 411 64 50 90.

Modern Art Visit www.modernartinc.com or call +44 (0)20 8980 7742 for Conceptual, Minimalist, and Modern sculpture and art.

The New Art Centre The garden of the private country house at Roche Court provides the setting for this sculpture park (and gallery) that displays a variety of high-quality sculpture for sale. Based in the south of England, it specializes in work from 1950 onwards, displaying some of the best names in British sculpture, and is the sole representative of the estate of Barbara Hepworth. Visit www.sculpture.uk.com or call +44 (0)1980 862 244 for further information.

Robert Bowman Gallery This gallery in London specializes in bronze, marble, and terracotta sculpture from the 19th century to the present day, including animalia. Visit www.robertbowman.com or call +44 (0)20 7839 3100.

Rupert Wace Rupert deals in ancient Egyptian, classical, and near Eastern sculpture from his gallery in London, and shows at art fairs internationally. Visit www.rupertwace.co.uk or call +44 (0)20 7495 1623.

Sladmore Gallery This London gallery, off Berkeley Square, specializes in animalia and has frequent exhibitions. They have increasingly concentrated on fine casts of 19th- and early 20th-century bronzes, as well as representing a small stable of contemporary artists. Visit www.sladmore.com or call +44 (0)20 7499 0365.

Sculpture in the South This is a show of figurative sculpture from around the world in May each year in Summerville, South Carolina, in the United States. Visit www.sculptureinthesouth.com or call +1 843 851 7800 for more information.

Timothy Gallery Contemporary sculpture can be found at Timothy Taylor's London gallery. Visit www.timothygallery.com.

World Sculpture News A magazine published in Hong Kong but distributed in Europe and North America. Visit www.worldsculpturenews.com or call Hong Kong on +852 2522 3443.

HOW TO GET THE BEST DEALS

"Art in its perfection is not ostentatious, it lies hid and works its effect, itself unseen."
Joshua Reynolds

What you will learn in this chapter:

- How to ensure you invest well, minimizing the risks
- How to ensure you achieve a reasonable price
- The importance of provenance
- Advice on which fields are currently worth investing in
- Where to find bargains

With an increasing number of art shows and galleries springing up, you want to ensure that the money you spend on a work of art is well spent. Thanks to the Internet, where you can see sale prices for thousands of works of art at the click of a button, it is now easy and quick to check prices by consulting one of the online price guides (*see* Useful Contacts & Reference, p.20) or books such as the *Miller's Pictures Price Guide*. Unfortunately, this means that *everyone* is now more aware of what kind of prices art is capable of fetching, and will rarely undersell anything. It has therefore become increasingly difficult to find works by good artists for next to nothing. It also means that there are many overpriced artworks out there: simply looking at the prices that a few works by an artist have fetched is a very inaccurate way of judging the value of a piece of art because prices for one person's work can vary wildly (*see* What Affects the Price of Art, p.13). Just as in any field of investment, once you have paid money for something there is no guarantee that its value will increase; in fact, if an artist goes out of fashion prices might even drop. However, as any investment consultant will tell you, there are things you can do to minimize the risks, and these are detailed below.

HOW TO INVEST WISELY

Know the field As I have said previously, knowledge of the field in which you are buying is the key. This means that it is best to specialize. You can of course collect across different periods and styles, but you will find it harder to buy wisely if you are armed only with a scant knowledge of the subject.

Do not confuse affordable with cheap Affordable means good-quality works at reasonable prices, rather than cheap. As we have seen, fashion can affect the price of art, so affordability is often just a matter of timing. A piece that is undervalued today because an artist's work is out of fashion, despite his or her work once being critically acclaimed and examples being held in major museums, may represent an affordable purchase. If the only reason for the decline in value of an artist's work is the capriciousness of the buying public and a constant barrage of information telling you about the next big thing or vogue then it may be a wise choice to purchase at this point. Of course it is a risk, but as long as you are confident that the works are of intrinsically high quality there is always a good chance that trends will go full circle and prices will increase again – the old maxim "speculate to accumulate" applies here.

Following fashion (rather than setting or awaiting it), on the other hand, never makes you money. Turn the Internet to your advantage and use all the facilities available to view price trends. If a high-quality artist with excellent provenance is going down in value it might be a good idea to buy, keep for a while, and sell when art dealers and the public re-evaluate the artist. One of the artists that dealer Robert Sandelson represents is a case in point: Bridget Riley is an internationally recognized British Op Artist, important and fêted; she has appeared in books and had shows at important museums. But five years ago the spotlight turned away from her for a while so you could buy her very best work for £15,000 ($24,000), and prints and smaller works for much less, perhaps as little as £300 ($480). Today, however, her good pictures sell for hundreds of thousands, and smaller works and prints fetch £2,000–£3,000 ($3,600–$5,400). Collectors who took their chances and bought her work five years ago could now profit considerably. Mid-20th-century artist Ivon Hitchens is another example – in eight years his work has increased in price nearly five-fold. Dealers saw that these artists were unfashionable and therefore undervalued, so bought up their work and kept it until they returned to the public eye.

Understand how art rises in value There are various reasons for this, including an improving economy, the influence of auctions and dealers, and the publicity of exhibitions, books, and good marketing. Refer back to chapter two (pp.22–28) to remind yourself of these, and aim to make educated assumptions rather than speculating wildly.

Discover the "radar line" Excellent work can be found under what dealers call the "radar line". Below a certain price (the radar line) wealthy collectors are often not interested. Since they make their money in other areas, top-end collectors do not speculate much in art. They can afford the "best" – the most sought-after pictures by world-famous names. Many of these collectors buy the best to boast that they can. Besides, big names may cost millions but they increase in value by millions too. Sadly, most of us cannot afford to spend the price of a nice house on a picture, so we have to look below the radar line. Happily, as such collectors seem to apply the rule that if a picture is above a certain price it must be good, this leaves many excellent works of art available to the less wealthy at much lower prices.

Check records The first thing to do is to check the auction house's records for where the piece was bought, or if buying from an individual or a gallery, ask if they have any receipts or sales dockets. This will help you to assess whether you are being charged a reasonable price. All respectable galleries write out receipts, so if you know that a certain picture was sold by a certain gallery it is reassuring. Likewise, a picture must have a certain merit for an auction house to take it. Knowing where a piece came from also contributes to your knowledge of its provenance (*see* below).

When buying an artist at a first-time show you have no previous prices to compare with, so just pay the price if you can afford it and take your chance. The gallery owner can't charge very high prices for a previously unshown artist anyway.

Look closely Always inspect a piece of artwork carefully before buying, in order to check its condition. A flaking oil or a foxed print is not a good investment (*see* What Affects the Price of Art, p.13, and p.59). A chipped or damaged modern sculpture is not a good investment either, and a sculpture from 4,000 years ago in perfect condition is very rare and maybe a bit suspicious – it could be a fake.

PROVENANCE

Provenance is the history and documentation relating to an artist – mainly referring to the line of previous owners of a work of art – and is an important factor to consider when buying (*see also* How to Minimize the Chance of Buying a Fake, p.134). If there is provenance the work automatically has greater investment potential.

When thinking about buying an artist's work, the questions you need to ask include:

If the artist is living, where has he or she shown before? If they have shown in an important institution or have had one-person, rather than group, shows that means they are more well-known. **Is work by the artist in a museum or a private or corporate collection?** If their work is, or has been, in a good public or private collection it will automatically have a higher value than those whose work has not. Although it is not widely known, for the past 50 years the Arts Council of Great Britain has had a yearly budget of around £150,000 to purchase the work of living artists. They do not just focus on a few artists, but aim to represent all fields. They currently hold over 7,500 pieces – paintings, sculptures, original works on paper, artists' prints, photographs, and film and video installations – and are collecting all the time. Buyers are appointed for an 18-month period only, so tastes are varied. These artists represent investment potential. You can find out about them in books published for the Hayward Gallery in London, starting with *Arts Council Collection Acquisitions 1989–2002*, by Isobel Johnstone. Many corporations in the United States buy art by inexpensive living artists they believe in. Because of budgetary concerns they would rather buy good art cheaply than wait until the pieces become expensive. Consequently, however, being bought by a big corporation may raise the prices of an artist's work by giving it the valued provenance of being owned by a well-known company.

If the artist is dead who is the seller? A reputable auction house or dealer is preferable to a private seller in order to avoid being sold a fake or a bad-quality piece. Backing by a reputable dealer or an auction house gives added value to a picture.

Who owned the work of art before? It can add value to the artwork if the previous owner is well known. An extreme example of this is a batch of boring watercolours that belonged to the Duchess of Windsor, which fetched ten times or more than their estimates. The exorbitant price that was paid for the Picasso too (*see* p.12) must have been helped, in part, by its belonging to one of America's premier families, the Whitneys, especially as the auction house publicized the fact. Libraries and archives like those at the Courtauld Institute in London can prove useful when researching the provenance of works of art (*see* Useful Contacts and Reference, p.110).

AFFORDABLE FIELDS TO CONSIDER NOW

The following fields are currently affordable, and have growth potential:

Irish art As we have seen, economic growth seems to generate nationalist sentiments, which may be expressed in buying works of art. This is why, following strong all-round economic growth, anything Irish has risen hugely over the past few years, particularly good-quality portraits, which no one expected.

Russian art The citizens of the former Soviet Union, always nationalistic, wish to spend their new disposable incomes on Russian art. So if you find an inexpensive, good-quality Russian work in a tiny gallery in Britain or the United States, smuggled out after the Revolution and sold by émigrés, you could buy it, then put it into auction in London or New York and probably make a profit. Previously only Sotheby's offered a sale of Russian art, but Christie's have now inaugurated their first Russian sale. This is, therefore, an area of growing interest.

Contemporary Chinese art Shanghai now hosts two contemporary art fairs and has a well-respected Contemporary Art museum. Most of the record prices fetched at the fairs have been for European works – Picassos and casts of Rodin sculptures – which were bought by businesses. However, more galleries selling Chinese art are opening all the time. The Shanghai International Art Festival, sponsored by the Chinese Ministry of Culture, and the huge Shanghai Art Fair run at the same time, the latter being an important trading place. Many buyers are attracted by a style known as Political Pop, which is being bought mostly by foreigners at the moment. For Western collectors it combines the familiar with the exotic. On the whole, the market in Chinese contemporary art is relatively undeveloped and so is a good place for investment, given the recent growth of those with a disposable income in the country.

American contemporary and 1960s art According to ArtPrice.com, American artists who worked in the 1960s are fetching record prices today. Many have become beyond the reach of most buyers, so it is a good idea either to buy limited-edition prints of Pollock, Rothko, and Lichtenstein, or to learn about other artists. The British 60s artist Bridget Riley has already been taken up (*see* p.100), so look for others that were respected in their time but are less familiar now, as they may be set to rise in price in the future.

Outsider art Marcel Duchamp championed what was labelled as "Art Brut" ("Outsider Art") by French writer Jean Dubuffet. Writing in the 1940s, Dubuffet contended that "art by artists with art school training is lifeless by virtue of the praise heaped upon it." He felt that true art was to be found in unlikely places, such as psychiatric hospitals and prisons, among people distanced from high culture by their lack of education and their remoteness from the art establishment. Sixty years later, Outsider Art is a flourishing collectors' market with an annual art fair in New York and specialist dealers in London. The American Visionary Museum in Baltimore is devoted entirely to Outsiders. Most of the work is on scraps of paper in crayon or pencil, as other materials are too expensive or unavailable to the artists on the edge of society, and the work is often intricate.

Only a few years ago Outsider Art could be picked up very cheaply, but artists such as Canadian-born Scottie Wilson, whose pictures often depict the battle between good and evil, are now sought after. Such work is now going for over £2,000 ($3,600) – not a fortune, but as a market is currently being generated the work could well rise in price even further.

Mexican art Adrian Searle, art critic of British newspaper *The Guardian*, believes that a portrait by self-taught native Indian artist Hermenegildo Bustos (1832–1907) is as good as any by any modern European painter working at the same time. Indeed, when a portrait of Bustos' wife was hanging in an exhibition in Lille, Searle felt that it was better than the Modigliani bust of a woman opposite it. Bustos is rather cheaper than Modigliani, so this may well be worth looking into.

Diego Rivera was one of Mexico's greatest artists – and Frida

Kahlo's husband – and his name is now becoming better known to Europeans. His work is still inexpensive if compared to Picasso or Mondrian, both of whom he knew. He experimented with Cubism, as did Picasso, and had a studio in the same building as Mondrian. However, Diego Rivera's work is no longer cheap, so if your budget does not stretch that far it may be an idea to look for an artist who is less well known, but who perhaps influenced him in Europe or Mexico.

Symbolism With so much art today reflecting the media and the technological age, collectors may well become interested in the more esoteric oils, chalk and pencil sketches, and lithographs of the Symbolists (*see* p.181). Aside from the big names, such as Odilon Redon and Gustave Moreau, there were also less well-known, and thus more affordable, artists working in Scandinavia and eastern Europe.

ARTISTS ASSOCIATED WITH FAMOUS NAMES

A good way of finding affordable art with high investment potential is to investigate the artists who taught the big names, or whom they themselves taught. As the well-respected masters become beyond many people's price range, collectors naturally start to look at those artists who surrounded them.

WHERE TO FIND BARGAINS & SELL AT THE BEST PRICE

Although there are minimum price guidelines for most works of art it is still possible to find works that have been undervalued for one reason or another. You are more likely to find a work at a lower than average price from an auction house or dealer whose clientele are interested in other types of art. For example, a relative of a recently deceased artist may allow an antique dealer to buy their relative's dining table on the condition that they buy everything else, including the pictures. The antique dealer interested in the table will know clients who want to buy furniture, but may not know ones who want pictures. Therefore the pictures will probably be sold at the recommended minimum value so that the auctioneer can get rid of them quickly. Similarly, let's say you find a Cubist picture of a New York skyline in an English provincial auction house. It stands to reason that it will go for considerably less than it would if it were offered for sale in Manhattan – another bargain!

The same principle applies if you are selling – it is always best to sell through a dealer who specializes in what you are wishing to sell. What you are selling may be area-dependent too. For example, if you have a horse picture it is far better to sell it at an auction house in a part of the country that is interested in horses, so the countryside is a better option than a large city.

I know of someone who makes a good living by buying from provincial general auction houses and then selling through the Internet on eBay. While the competing bidders he contends with when buying at the provincial auction number a few hundred, those bidding on eBay to buy his stock potentially number a few million, resulting in a substantial gain.

HIDDEN MASTERPIECES

It is rare – thanks to all the television shows encouraging us to get our things valued – but still possible, for masterpieces to emerge from granny's attic. Recently the Tate Gallery in London launched an appeal to trace 400 paintings by J.M.W. Turner that have gone missing since he painted them. Of course some have been lost through fire and flood, but many are still in hiding somewhere in the world. According to experts, one or two interesting Turners turn up every year. Not long ago a Turner was found in a car boot sale in New Zealand, and subsequently was sold for a great deal of money at auction. A few years ago a Turner watercolour view of Lausanne, which specialists had no idea existed, was exhibited. Before that a whole Turner sketchbook surfaced from a private collection. The owners had an inkling that the sketches were by Turner, but had not bothered to get them authenticated.

So why are there missing masterpieces? Often it is because an ancestor bought a picture by a famous artist from a friend, so there was no paperwork, or from a dealer but the verification has long since been lost. Collecting may have been a private passion of the ancestor so he did not bother to tell his children or his wife, who were probably not interested anyway. The upshot is that, two or three generations later, the family do not know what they have because their parents never knew. When a new generation moves into a house that has remained in the family they often refurbish in their own taste and put their parents' pictures in a barn or outhouse: recently two Canalettos materialized from a barn near Bristol. A Constable was also found in a routine house valuation in Essex – it had been in the possession of the artist's lawyer, whose descendants had obviously forgotten about their antecedent's famous client.

Of course some work just goes out of fashion and temporarily prices tumble (see p.24). Journalist and art expert Martin Gayford recalls how a piece called *Dancing Faun* by the Renaissance sculptor Adriaen de Vries made headlines when it was found at a run-of-the-mill garden sculpture auction. It had been part of a job lot of apparently undistinguished pieces sold in the 1950s for a few guineas. Forty years later the piece sold for £7 million ($11.2 million). Buyers in the 1950s probably knew that the sculpture was a de Vries, but didn't care because he was wildly unpopular at the time.

Some dealers specialize in trawling auction houses for undiscovered masterpieces, or "sleepers" as they are known in the trade. They might buy a picture catalogued as Venetian School on the hunch that it will later turn out to be a Titian. Not surprisingly, the sellers of such pieces get very upset when they find out they have missed out on the huge financial gain they could have made. Sometimes the auction house will offer recompense for overlooking a masterpiece, but not always. In

1987 the original owner of a Sebastiano del Piombo did receive out-of-court damages from Sotheby's for such a loss: he had received only £180 ($270) for the piece at auction in Chester, after which it was resold by the dealer for £330,000 ($490,000) to another dealer who then sold it on to the Getty Museum in California for £6.5 million ($9.5 million).

IS IT BEST TO BUY AT HOME OR ABROAD?

As Europe has the *droit de suite* system (*see* chapter one, p.19) you may be wondering if there are advantages to buying in one country over another. The United States and Australia have no *droit de suite* system, and no plans to introduce one, so you may deduce that you could get a better deal in those countries. However, there are other factors to take into consideration too:

Currency A purchase made in a country with a relatively weak currency can yield unexpected savings. For example, at the time of writing the pound sterling is fairly strong in comparison with the US dollar. All paintings bought in the United States therefore seem cheaper to British buyers.

Supply and demand If there is a large supply of a certain type of art in one country or part of the world it is best to buy there as the number of examples available keeps the prices to their minimum. For example, Europe wins hands down over America when it comes to Old Masters and Old Master Drawings. So New York dealers often buy in Europe and sell in New York. The same can be said of good, inexpensive French and British art, though art by big names is expensive anywhere. However, if you managed to find an American painter, such as Fairfield Porter or a member of the Hudson River School, in Europe, even though there may not be many of them it would certainly be cheaper because the competition for it in the UK is less. If you buy a view of an English landmark in the United States it could be cheaper, unless of course you are unlucky enough to be bidding against someone whose family originated from England.

De-nationalization of auction houses Until 2001 the French government owned its nation's auction houses, with auctioneers being officers of the state. This is no longer the case, and foreign auction houses are now allowed to trade in France. There has consequently been a rise in art sales in the country, thanks to competitive commissions between the auction houses and a wider range of potential buyers from around the world. More choice and sales attract more competitive buyers, who push prices up. Now it is only in Belgium and Denmark that auction houses are under state control.

Transport and export costs You should always bear in mind the cost of shipping pieces from abroad, and make sure that it does not add significantly to the whole cost of the piece, making it less cost efficient.

USEFUL CONTACTS & REFERENCE

See previous chapters and the Directory on p.183 for other useful contacts and reference, such as the auction records websites on p.20.

Arts Council and the Hayward Gallery Arts Council England is the national development agency for the arts in England, distributing public money from the government and the National Lottery. It supports the Hayward Gallery on the South Bank of the Thames. Visit www.artscouncil.org.uk or call +44 (0)845 300 6200. For the Hayward Gallery visit www.hayward.org.uk (where you can also find the publishing details for *Arts Council Collection Acquisitions*) or call +44 (0)20 7960 5226.

SHIPPING

There are also shipping and packaging firms on pp.160–1 (Cadogan Tate and Gander & White), and on p.170 (Fine Art Shipping and Northern Artery).

Art Move This UK-based company transports art worldwide by sea and air. They also offer specialist art installation (from hanging a single picture to a full public exhibition) and storage services. Visit www.artmove.co.uk or call +44 (0)20 7585 1801.

EuroUSA These shippers specialize in inter-continental shipping and offer a door-to-door service. They are perfectly capable of shipping works of art between countries and will organize tax matters. No European tax is paid on sales commissions for export; tax, if applicable, is paid in the country of destination. Price is based on cubic volume. Visit www.the-eurogroup.com or call in the UK on +44 (0)1638 515 335 or in the United States on +1 301 483 8667.

RESEARCHING PROVENANCE

Christie's archives It is free to visit Christie's archives in London, and they have sale catalogues going back many years so you can check and compare prices of artists. To visit the archive department in the King Street salerooms, make an appointment on +44 (0)20 7389 2617.

Conway Library A division of the Courtauld Institute at Somerset House, London, containing records of sculpture sold at exhibitions and auctions. The records contain many thousands of sculptors and over a million pieces made by them. The library is open to all, but membership is required along with a small charge. Visit www.courtauld.ac.uk or call +44 (0)207 848 2782 for further details

Witt Library Adjacent to the Conway Library, this houses an archive of exhibition and auction house catalogues and some specialist journals covering paintings from AD 1200 to the present day – 1.9 million images by 77,000 international artists are held. It is necessary to become a member but this is open to all. A small charge is levied. Visit www.courtauld.ac.uk or call +44 (0)207 848 2743.

CHINESE ART

International Shanghai Arts Festival A multiplicity of arts disciplines is showcased at this event. Visit www.artsbird.com.
Shanghai Art Fair For information on this fair visit www.sartfair.com, where individual exhibiting galleries and their contact details are listed, or call +86 21 6225 4977.

MEXICAN ART

Galeria Louis Morton This gallery in Chapultepec, Mexico, sells very interesting Mexican art. Visit www.lmorton.com or call +52 5520 5005.

OUTSIDER ART

American Visionary Museum Visit the attractive website at www.avam.org or call +1 410 244 1900.
Moscow Museum of Outsider Art The first ever Russian Museum of Outsider Art, which opened in 1996. It remains dedicated exclusively to collecting and exhibiting Outsider Art in Russia. Visit www.museum.ru/outsider or call +7 095 465 6304.
Outsider Art Fair 35 dealers gather for this fair in New York in January. For further information visit www.sanfordsmith.com/out.html or call Lana Zepponi at Sanford L. Smith Associates on +1 212 777 5218.

RUSSIAN ART

Bukowski's There are a lot of Russian émigrés in Finland, and Helsinki-based auction house Bukowski's sees many Russian paintings coming up for sale. Visit www.bukowskis.fi or call +358 9 6668 9110.

HOW & WHERE TO BUY ART

"Entry free – with hands in pockets.
Exit easy – with picture under arm."
André Breton

What you will learn in this chapter:
- How to buy through a dealer and how to find the best dealer for you
- How to buy at auction
- The role art agents play and how to buy from them
- How to buy from the Internet and avoid the pitfalls
- How to buy from degree shows

There are two traditional choices: do you buy and sell through the auction house, or do you go through a dealer, or "gallerist" as dealers now like to call themselves (at their gallery or at an art fair)? Then there are the Internet, degree shows, and art agents. It is good to know what to expect, whichever one you to decide to buy from.

BUYING THROUGH A DEALER

You may have to pay more when using a dealer, but this is often worth it as you are also buying advice and knowledge that will benefit you in the future. When you part with your hard-earned money for a work of art you want to feel that you are making a good investment, that the artist is good and their work will at least retain its value. A dealer can give you assurances because he or she has researched the artist and believes in them, which they prove by giving them an exhibition or risking their money by buying a certain artist's work.

Dealers can help you buy wisely: as a would-be collector you should encourage the dealer to talk, and listen to what they say. Dealers will always share their knowledge with someone who is genuinely interested, although their antennae are pretty finely tuned to detect time-wasters or show-offs, so never pretend you can afford more than you can. They will like you to have done a bit of research beforehand, too, and do not warm to the approach of "Show me everything, I'll know what I like when I see it." They may do it once but the next time they will not waste their time so easily.

However, when buying from a dealer you should also remember that they have the gift of the gab, and many are very smart salespeople. One of the most famous art dealers of the 20th century was Lord Duveen, who employed some clever tricks to get people to buy. One of the most famous stories about him concerns an impatient Chicago millionaire collector, whom he kept waiting for two hours before hurrying him through a room full of Dutch Old Masters. They were far too expensive, explained Duveen. Indignant at the implication that he could not afford the pictures, the millionaire bought the lot!

PRIVATE VIEWS

If you are genuinely interested in a particular type of art, a dealer may ask you to a private view at the gallery. This is when special clients have access by invitation, giving them a chance to buy before the general public see the works of art. A private view is a good place to meet people who share your interests, and again you could gain invaluable knowledge from them.

HELP WITH PURCHASES

In a pioneering move, the Arts Council of England (see Useful Contacts & Reference, p.127) now offers interest-free loans of up to £2,000 ($3,600) for the purchase of works by living English artists. The work(s) have to be bought from one (or more) of 250 galleries participating in the scheme. All you need to do is go to one of the galleries and choose something you like, or some galleries will help you commission something unique by an artist you admire, and then apply for the loan. The scheme is also being extended so that art schools and colleges will be able to offer "Own Art" at their degree shows, making an excellent opportunity to discover, and buy, new talent. If you are successful you will repay in instalments by standing order. You may be asked for a 10 per cent deposit by the gallery, but if your application is unsuccessful the deposit will be returned. The scheme is also available in Scotland, from the Scottish Arts Council. Hopefully similar schemes will be set up elsewhere.

ART FAIRS

The number of art fairs has increased enormously over the past few years. Dealers may complain that they don't sell much there, but do not imagine that you will get a bargain as a result. Dealers use art fairs to attract new customers and put work into a competitive situation. One gallerist recalls how a client could not make up her mind about a sculpture in the showroom, but when she saw it at an art fair she panicked because she thought someone else would buy it. She admitted that she made the purchase essentially to prevent anyone else having the piece. Art fairs are not always the best place to buy art as pieces are displayed close together, the lighting is not always ideal, and there is so much to choose from. However, art fairs are excellent places to compare and contrast prices and styles, and to acquire knowledge through conversations with gallerists who are usually willing to talk to potential new clients.

If you feel confused at an art fair, and like a painting or sculpture but are not 100 per cent sure, you could ask if you could take it home for the night after the fair closes and return it when it when the fair opens again in the morning. This is a much better approach than regretting an impulse purchase afterwards. You may have to leave a returnable deposit.

SELLING THROUGH A DEALER

It is a dealer's job to make a profit, so he or she will obviously buy from you at a price that is lower than they would sell at. Unscrupulous dealers might offer you considerably less, but this is risky because if you found out about any deceit then you would not sell or buy through them again. Reputable dealers want return business, so this does not happen very often.

You could offer a picture or sculpture on consignment, meaning that you leave the piece with the dealer who pays you when it is sold, at which time he or she will take a commission. But before consigning it is worth finding out about the dealer's reputation through others who have done business with him or her before. You need to know that they are the best choice for the particular work of art you wish to sell.

HOW DO YOU FIND A GOOD DEALER?

The relationship between client and dealer should develop into a very fulfilling one. When the dealer knows what you collect he or she will be able to source items, so take your time to find the dealer who is right for you.

Do not go to a hobby dealer – that is to say, someone who is an art dealer on the side. This kind of person may run a shop in a seaside town with a few pretty pictures on the side in among furniture made of driftwood. You need to find a specialist in the field you are interested in.

Find out how long the dealer has been in business. If there are pieces you like, go in and chat to the dealer and find out a bit about them. You want to know their curriculum vitae – where they worked before and their area of expertise. What you must beware of is someone who has made money in a different field and thought it would be fun to start a gallery in a provincial town. Art dealing is not just "fun": it should be a passion and a business. A dealer should be hungry and devote all his or her energy to selling works of art.

Check to see if the dealer is a member of a trade association. Of course being a member of a trade association does not guarantee that the dealer is not involved in sharp practices (and there are also some very knowledgeable and reliable dealers who are not part of any association), but it is less likely. There are smart international trade associations, but there are also local ones. Nobody wants a crooked art dealer in their town, and a bad reputation spreads. If a dealer has more than five years trading under their belt it is likely that he or she will be pretty reputable, because the chances are somebody would have become aware of any dodgy dealings during that time.

There are some other points to check out before selling through a dealer:

Insurance What kind of insurance does the gallery have if your picture becomes damaged on their premises?

Legal position If a gallery were to go bankrupt with your property on consignment it is worth checking what your position would be with a lawyer specializing in art (see Useful Contacts & Reference, chapter six, p.160–1).

Research It is a good idea to visit a number of dealers who specialize in your chosen field to get an idea of the price you might be offered. Often the first question a dealer asks is, "So how much do you want for it?" You should also do research through books or auction records, ensuring that you compare like with like, before accepting an offer.

HOW DEALERS CHARGE

Dealers can be rather coy about their charges, because they will always do deals. If you are buying from an exhibition, your ability to negotiate depends on the success of the show. If, after the private view and the week following, few of the pieces have sold, then you are in a strong negotiating position. If on the other hand only one work remains after the private view, then they will be disinclined to give you a discount.

When buying from archive stock, the best way of negotiating is to ask the dealer to give you his or her best price. You then tell them whether it is acceptable or not. However, negotiating on works of art is not akin to a Moroccan souk. Art dealers do not like being beaten down and beaten down – the next time they will simply start at a higher price. The dealer-buyer relationship should be an honest and giving one. One party should not try to outdo the other.

Contrary to what you may believe, dealers do not carry huge stock. However, they can usually find the pieces you want by calling on a few colleagues – this is called the secondary market. The primary market is when the dealer is the sole agent for a particular artist.

When selling through a dealer the percentage price he or she marks up on your piece can depend on how quickly it can be sold. Fast turnover is always desirable, as no one wants stock hanging about for years. A dealer will vary their commission depending on the piece. So for expensive and desirable paintings the mark-up could be as little as 10 per cent, but for work that is probably going to be around for a while, gathering dust in a back room while waiting for the right buyer, the mark-up could rise to 30 or 40 per cent. Expect the commission to be 15 to 20 per cent for most works of art.

BUYING AT AUCTION

For buyers, auction houses offer the potential of finding an undiscovered bargain. There are always stories about an Old Master that was thought to be an undistinguished Victorian copy being bought at a country auction for pittance, which then turns out to be worth a fortune. These finds are very rare, but nevertheless do happen because in sales outside large cities huge volumes of furniture, pictures, sculpture, and every kind of antique find their way to auction, and the experts cannot know everything. Equally, in the large auction houses with specialist departments there are not the time or the resources to give painstaking individual attention to each and every piece.

For the new collector auctions can be a good starting place. Prices at auction are often around 20 per cent lower than through a dealer, although this is by no means a hard and fast rule. An auction depends on competition, and if there are many people competing for one painting, prices can rocket. However, as you are bound to make some mistakes when first buying, with an auction house you can always put it back into a sale.

There is one caveat about buying at auction – it is known as "the Ring". This is when a group of dealers bid you up because they do not want you to establish a lower price for the object, and they then pull out. This is of course strictly illegal, but hard to prove.

Nowadays, because auction houses sell to the public as well as to dealers, estimates are published in their catalogues. They take the form of two figures between which the piece may sell. Auction houses do often estimate lower than the eventual figure reached, because it pleases the vendor more if their work of art sells for more than they had expected and of course it would be very disappointing to receive less money than anticipated. The reserve (the price below which the owner is unwilling to sell) equals the lowest estimate. When a work of art fails to reach its reserve the auction house will not sell it. The term used here is "bought in".

There is a lot of information in the front and back of auction catalogues, albeit in small print. The buyer's premium (see How Auctions Charge, p.120) is listed here, and so are the numbers for telephone and fax bidding and the address of where to send your absentee bid form (see Absentee Bidding, p.122).

It is now possible to view the lots in a sale in colour over the Internet. Even the traditional auction houses have websites.

SELLING AT AUCTION

Auction houses are much better places to sell when you have pieces that have never been seen on the market before. The value can only be determined by putting them on the open market. Recently Christie's sold a lot of photos by Joseph-Philibert Girault de Prangey that made far more than most dealers would have ever expected. Auctions can attract buyers beyond the dealers' address books.

However, it is always best to see an item in the flesh, in case there are any flaws – tiny scratches or minute chips in a picture's frame, for example – that do not show up in the photograph.

The price you will get at auction is governed entirely by who is there to compete for the work.

HOW DO YOU CHOOSE AN AUCTION HOUSE?

If you had a picture believed to be a Gainsborough and you wanted to sell it, it would not be advisable to sell through a provincial auction house, far away from major transport links. You want to make it easy for as many people as possible to attend the auction. The easier it is to get to, the more people will come and bid. The "big three" auction houses – Bonhams, Christie's, and Sotheby's – have an international mailing list. They also have more money for press and publicity and will give parties to promote the art in a major city where they think the picture will sell.

When choosing between the big three, it really comes down to individual taste and personal preference. If you have a very desirable piece, visit all three and consider which one offers the best service in terms of reaching as many people's notice as possible. If you are selling a collection, have a look at how the catalogue would be produced. It should look good and be well written. A good-looking catalogue can also enhance the value of an individual object in a collection.

These criteria can be applied to smaller auctioneers, too, and although Bonhams, Christie's, and Sotheby's have offices in the major cities of Europe and North America, there are vast areas of the world where they have no presence.

If you live in an area where the big three are not represented, you might be better off going to a local auction house with a good local reputation – it may even be more appropriate. For example, if you live in Kentucky, why bother to send equestrian art to New York? Much better to sell it locally in this horse-racing area. Sometimes, even if there is a big three representative but not an auction house, as in some smaller cities, it would be best to go to an actual auction house. For example, Sotheby's may have an office in Dublin, but the city boasts the very good auction house Whytes, which has achieved record prices for Irish art. You can find out about local auctioneers in the *International Directory of Arts* (*see* Useful Contacts & Reference, p.126).

HOW AUCTIONS CHARGE

Buyers and sellers are charged between 10 and 20 per cent. The "big three" charge nearer 20 per cent, while provincial houses in the United States and the UK tend to charge less. However, it may be possible to negotiate a lower seller's commission. After the scandal of price-fixing involving Sotheby's and Christie's in the 1990s, auction houses are especially keen to appear competitive. If what you are selling can bring publicity and prestige to the auction house, then they could well bring down commission to get you to sell through them. As regards tax, this is charged only on their commission and not on the whole value of the work.

BIDDING AT AUCTION

When at auction I am always terrified that an involuntary movement, such as a cough, will attract the auctioneer's attention and unwittingly make me a bidder for something I do not want. However, the major auction houses now issue paddles with numbers on them, which you can acquire on request before the sale. You will probably also be put through a credit check to ensure you have no bad debts and can pay for your lot. You are given a bidder number that corresponds with the paddle. This method avoids signal mix-ups and the problem of the auctioneer not hearing your name properly (gone are the days when you shouted out your name across the room). Raise your paddle so it is visible when you want to start bidding, hold it there, then drop it when you want to quit. Unfortunately not all auction houses employ paddles. If you are buying in one without them keep your signals simple. Raise your hand when you want to enter the bidding and once the auctioneer knows you are in the game he or she will look to you when it is your turn to continue or stop. Nod your head to continue and shake it to pull out.

An auctioneer will often start off the bidding below the reserve price to encourage buyers. If no one puts their hand up the auctioneer is allowed to bid on behalf of the seller to raise the bid to the reserve. However, in the United States an auctioneer is not allowed to bid against himself or another person in the room more than three times to reach the reserve. He or she warns the bidder by saying "against you Sir/Madam".

WHEN SHOULD YOU ENTER AN AUCTION?

Obviously if the lot you want is one of the last of the day then there is no need to arrive early in the morning. Approximately 100 lots are covered in an hour, so time your arrival accordingly. When to enter the bidding is more difficult to decide. Some buyers like to enter early, especially if the pace of sale is irregular, as they feel they might miss something otherwise. They like to start the bidding because it makes them feel in control. The advantage of coming in at the last minute, when the auctioneer is saying "going, going", is that it can confuse the person you are bidding against, who might be thrown off kilter and lose concentration because he thinks that the goods are already his.

ABSENTEE BIDDING

It is possible to bid over the telephone. The procedure is as follows: you leave your telephone number (mobile/cell or landline) and the lot number you want with the absentee bids department, and someone will call you three or so lots before yours. You are then listening to the auctioneer and when it is your lot you are invited to bid remotely. If you are worried that you might be on another call or out of telephone reception range, then you can leave what is called an emergency bid. This is the top price you are prepared to pay.

An absentee bid can also be in the form of a written bid, using an "absentee bid form", which can usually be found in the back of the catalogue or downloaded from auction houses' websites. A member of staff will try to secure the piece for you at the lowest price possible. On the form you specify your maximum bid amount, then usually fax it to the bid department of the saleroom location to reach them at least 24 hours before the auction. By a similar process, absentee bids are also now sometimes available online.

HOW TO PAY & COLLECT

If you have become the proud new owner of a work of art, arrange to pay for it by credit card or cheque and collect it either at the end of the sale or within the next few days. Auction houses do charge for holding sold items. The period of time that they will give you for free storage varies, although it is mostly from a couple of days to a week. This gives you time to collect if you are coming from a distance, or to have enough time to arrange another person or carrier to pick up your goods.

ART AGENTS

A new player in the art world is emerging – the art agent.
Timothy Sammons, based in London, styles himself as an art
agent and sees his role as a negotiator who represents the
interests of one party, not of both. He maintains that the loyalty
of an auction house is divided between the seller, who wants
the highest price, and the buyer, who wants a bargain.

Sammons claims to be totally impartial, saying he will find
the best deal for his client, whether it is selling through an
auction or a private dealer (whoever, in his opinion, can achieve
the highest price for a work). One of his recent typical clients
thought that the painting in his attic was a portrait of Jane
Austen, but he could not be sure. He enlisted Sammons to do
an in-depth authentication, which often an auction house does
not have time to do. If enough people can verify a piece's
authenticity then Sammons will give possible high and low
prices. When the work is sold he will also help with the tax
implications (*see* Useful Contacts & Reference, p.129).

You can also buy through an art agent. They will locate
specific items for their clients and help form art collections. They
can also give advice on conservation of prospective purchases.

Sammons will not disclose his charges because he says he
tailors them to each client, but they don't come cheaply –
he says if a piece turns out to be worth less than £10,000
($18,000) it is not worth engaging his services. Where an art
agent is very useful is if you think you might have a masterpiece
hidden in your attic and want to get the best price for it. Always
find out an agent's charges before engaging them. No doubt
there will soon be many more people offering this service.

BUYING ON THE INTERNET

The number of Internet auction sites (*see* useful Contacts &
Reference, p.128) is increasing all the time in the wake of the
success of eBay, which lists up to 2.5 million private auctions in

the art and antiques section. The most common way of buying on Internet sites is known as the English auction method: the lot goes to the highest bidder at the end of a fixed period of time. There is no doubt that the Internet has revolutionized auctions, as more goods can be seen by more people. But technology brings its own problems, and buying on the Internet should definitely be viewed with caution. Firstly, the phrase "buyer beware" springs to mind. Although sellers should be honest, the onus is on the buyer to choose wisely. Obviously if you live in London you are not going fly to Miami to view a $300 picture that you might not get anyway, so you have to assess the risks and trust the seller. You can of course ask for documentation, but this could still be fraudulent (see chapter six, pp.138–40, for advice on online fraud).

There are two large sites dedicated to fine arts and antiques, iGavel.com and Bradstreets.com, both of them run by former auction house employees. Dealers or provincial auction houses can offer their wares to a much larger market through these two online auction houses. iGavel boasts of guarantees for authenticity and condition, and all the bidding is done online.

Registration is free on all reputable Internet sites. You simply go to the website, click on a button that usually says "Register", enter your details and a password, and follow the instructions on the screen.

All the online auction houses stagger closing times to compensate for different time zones, and the average bidding time is usually three weeks. Bradstreets has software in place that will automatically advance your bid to a pre-determined limit, and eBay offers a bidding-by-proxy system.

When you have got your lot there are usually various payment methods available, but it is advisable to opt for something like eBay's PayPal system, if available (see How to Safeguard Yourself Against Possible Online Fraud, p.139).

SELLING VIA THE INTERNET

First you have to register, then submit a good-quality photograph and a description of the item you wish to offer for consignment or sale. It is advisable to provide the best possible picture and most comprehensive description you can; this will help you to get the best price. If the buyer wants more pictures, provide them. Be willing to let him or her come round to see the art if they want to. Make it clear that there are postal/shipping charges on top of the sale price. On eBay it is important to get it into the right category. iGavel works slightly differently – they have fixed dates for items grouped together under appropriate categories; they will give you estimates, possible sale dates, and a suggested catalogue entry for your approval. iGavel is a site primarily for professional art dealers and small auction houses, but they welcome private individuals selling through these traders.

Like all regular auction houses, sellers can suggest a reserve (the minimum price that the vendor will accept). The starting bid at iGavel is the reserve. Bradstreets gives estimates and suggests that the first bid be two-thirds of the low estimate. On eBay you have to pay an Insertion Fee according to your starting price. If the item sells, you are then charged a percentage of the final price paid. As yet there is no seller's commission on iGavel and Bradstreets, just a small listing charge.

When you have sold via eBay wait for the buyer's payment to clear, which usually takes five working days if it is a cheque, before you send the artwork. On eBay you negotiate directly with the seller about shipping. iGavel arranges this for you – after an item is sold one of their associate dealers will collect payment on your behalf, arrange shipping, and send you the money minus these charges.

BUYING FROM AN ART SCHOOL OR COLLEGE DEGREE SHOW

In June each year, art school graduates in many parts of Europe and the United States hold degree shows to show off their work. These are great places to buy less expensive art, but you must accept that a purchase from one of these is purely speculative. The works are by artists at the beginning of their careers, and therefore immature. Unless they become big stars, their early work will not be as prized as their later and more accomplished pieces. The graduates may find they cannot cope with life as an artist, and after a short time embark on another career instead. Their early work will therefore not increase in value, because no dealer or auction house will be generating a market around them.

USEFUL CONTACTS & REFERENCE

International Directory of Arts A very useful three-volume annual directory listing art fairs, galleries, restorers, and auctioneers country by country. Published in Germany and translated into English, it is in most good public libraries. Currently in its 9th edition. (K.G. Saur Verlag, München, 2005.) Visit www.saur.de or call + 49 (0)89 769 02 300.

DEALERS

Antiques and Art Australia This website lists 200 commercial galleries and the areas in which they specialize, as well as art-related services including fairs and exhibitions, customs laws, art valuers or appraisers, and art magazines. Visit www.antique-art.com.au or contact John Furphy Pty Ltd, PO Box 8464, Armadale 3143, Victoria, Australia.

Art Dealers Association of America A New York-based, non-profit membership organization for the United States' leading galleries in the fine arts. Founded in 1962, it seeks to promote the highest standards and ethical practice within the profession. Recognized experts in prints and drawings. Visit www.artdealers.org or call +1 212 940 8590.

ArtDealerNet.com An online meeting place for art galleries, dealers, and collectors. You sign in for no charge with a request, and the site should link you to appropriate galleries. Appraising can be done online via ArtDealerNet, although I personally wouldn't recommend it, as it is impossible to judge condition over the Internet. Visit www.artdealernet.com.

British Antique Dealers Association A trade association for antique dealers in Britain whose main aim is to maintain high standards and to establish and maintain confidence between its members and the public. Browse their lists for dealers. Visit www.bada.org or call +44 (0)20 7589 4128.

The Fine Art Guild A good way of finding a reputable art dealer is to look at this London guild's list of members. They report on trade fairs and art-related news and information. Visit www.fineart.co.uk or call +44 (0)20 7381 6616.

Galleries This monthly magazine is a small but very useful booklet that lists all the major galleries in the UK with city maps included. It explains who is showing where and provides a brief description of the artist's work, with listings by area, specialization, and dealer. At the time of going to press a yearly subscription is £25 for the UK, or £35 ($60) for overseas. Visit www.artefact.co.uk or call/fax +44 (0)208 740 7020.

The National Antique & Art Dealers Association of America NAADAA is a non-profit trade association of America's leading dealers in antiques and works of art. Visit www.naadaa.org or call +1 212 826 9707.

Society of London Art Dealers This society lists 100 art dealers in London who have a proven reputation in their field and have signed an undertaking to observe standards of fair and honest dealing. Visit www.slad.org.uk or call +44 (0)20 7930 6137.

LOANS FOR ART

Arts Council of England Interest-free loans to buy contemporary English art are available from the Arts Council via a scheme called "Own Art". Visit www.artscouncil.org.uk, where you will find a list of participating galleries, or call +44 (0)845 300 6200. For the equivalent scheme in Scotland, visit the Scottish Arts Council's website at www.scottisharts.org.uk or call +44 (0) 131 226 6051.

FAIRS

(*See also* chapter one, Useful Contacts & Reference, p.21.)

The Affordable Art Fair This has become very popular, and there are now fairs in London, Bristol, Sydney, Melbourne, and New York. Prices range from £50 ($90) to £3,000 ($5,400). Visit www.affordableartfair.co.uk or call +44 (0)20 7371 8787.

Art Chicago Every May this international fair shows 2,500 plus emerging modern and contemporary artists. Visit www.artchicago.com or call +1 312 587 3300.

The International Fine Art Fair This New York fair held every May includes the *crème de la crème* of Western art. Visit www.haughton.com or call the London-based fair organizers on + 44 (0)20 7734 5491 or New York on +1 212 642 8572.

Scope Art Fairs These fairs are held in the Hamptons, New York, Miami, London, and Paris, and aim to bring together up-and-coming dealers, curators, and artists in a relaxed atmosphere. Visit www.scope-art.com or call +1 212 268 1522.

AUCTIONS

For full general contact details for the main auction houses please refer to the Directory on p.183.

American Society of Appraisers This organization is committed to fostering professional excellence in its membership through education, accreditation, publication, and other services. Visit www.appraisers.org or call +1 703 478 2228 to find accredited appraisers specializing in the fine arts.

Antiques Trade Gazette This well-established weekly trade newspaper lists auctions in London and the rest of the UK, along with important European ones. It also carries news on the state of the art market. Visit www.antiquestradegazette.com or call +44 (0)20 7420 6601.

National Auctioneers Association NAA member auctioneers are at the top of their field in the American auction business. Visit www.auctioneers.org or call +1 913 541 8084.

Online auctions Don't forget the websites discussed

previously: www.ebay.com (or ebay.co.uk, ebay.com.au, and so on), www.igavel.com, and www.bradstreets.com. eBay is the biggest and most famous auction site. However, buyer beware – unlike on specialist art sites the goods have not been looked over by an art professional.

Royal Institute of Chartered Surveyors – Arts and Antiques Faculty The RICS is one of the most respected and high profile global "standards and membership" organizations for professionals involved in land, property, construction, and environmental issues, including the valuation and auctioneering of fine art. For further information visit www.rics.org or call +44 (0)20 7222 7000.

Society of Fine Art Auctioneers This organization aims to ensure that its members throughout the UK maintain the highest standards of business practice and are transparent in their dealings. Visit www.sofaa.org or call +44 (0)1483 225 891.

ART AGENTS

Robert Holden Ltd The first to set up as an art agent in the UK, the company has over 20 years' experience advising private clients in the international art market. They are based at 15 Savile Row, London W1S 3PJ. Call +44 (0)20 7437 6010.

Timothy Sammons Fine Art This art agent has offices in London and New York. Visit www.timothy-sammons.com or call London on +44 (0)207 629 1386 or New York on +1 212 288 6806.

DEGREE SHOWS

Artschools.com An online art and design school directory for the USA and worldwide. This could help you find out about art schools in your area that might be having degree shows.

Degreeshow.com This website is a free service listing the UK Arts Degree Shows, as well as arts graduates and their details. Organized and sponsored by Candid Arts Trust. Visit www.degreeshow.com or call +44 (0)20 7837 4237.

BUYING THE GENUINE ARTICLE

"Where the spirit does not work with the hand there is no art." Leonardo da Vinci

What you will learn in this chapter:

- How forgeries can still be possible
- How to minimize the risks of buying a fake
- The significance of signatures, which can often provide clues in identifying fakes
- How to safeguard yourself against online fraud

With some works of art fetching millions, the temptation to fake them is greater than ever. Throughout the 1990s Londoner John Myatt forged works by major international artists on his kitchen table. At first he was very honest about his skills, putting an advertisement in a magazine that stated he had "Genuine Fakes for sale from £200". He received many requests and faked everything from Cubist paintings to Impressionist ones, as well as Dutch Old Masters. He even painted many Matisses using ordinary cheap house decorating paints! One day he received a call from a friend who said he had taken one of his works to Christie's, who had valued it as an important picture worth £25,000 ($40,000). The friend offered to split the profit with him. Unfortunately greed got the better of him, and from then on, with the help of accomplice John Drew, Myatt took his pictures to all the best dealers in London, where they were accepted as the real thing.

So how were these pictures accepted as genuine without provenance (*see* p.101)? Well, John Drew actually faked the provenances. He got a reader's ticket to the Tate Gallery library, but in art libraries he found it very difficult to remove papers of authenticity. It was not so difficult, however, to insert his own forged documents that verified pictures. Drew carefully used the same paper, typeface, and ink as those used on other bits of documentation referring to real pictures by the great artists themselves.

Drew and Myatt even fooled the Tate Gallery. They took a few pictures, again executed in ordinary emulsion paint, and were greeted with great respect. They were terrified and astounded when the pictures came back from the testing laboratory with a genuine certificate. Drew was caught only because his girlfriend informed the police, who tracked down Myatt too.

Recently, modern copies of the work of the 19th-century artist John Anster Fitzgerald (1823–1906) fooled art dealers. Fitzgerald's subjects were fairies set in surreal landscapes. The fakes were discovered only when the paint on them was examined and found not to have been available when Fitzgerald was painting. As in the case of Drew's and Myatt's fakes, the labels and provenance were cleverly duplicated and the wood and the board well distressed.

How many fakers are still out there, undiscovered, and how many collectors have pictures that are not by who they think they are? Probably quite a few.

FORGER: ELMYR DE HORY

One of the 20th century's best and most famous forgers was Elmyr de Hory (1906–76), thanks in part to the 1974 film *F for Fake,* made about him by Orson Welles. From the 1940s to the early 1960s he fooled the world's art connoisseurs, museums, and dealers with his frighteningly accurate copies of the work of Toulouse Lautrec, Picasso, Matisse, Vlaminck, Degas, and Modigliani. His fakes were sold as the real thing and de Hory made a great deal of money. After a spell in prison he began to paint his own work from his studio in Ibiza. His work – both his own and the identified fakes he made – is now very collectable, although they still cost considerably less than a real Matisse or Toulouse Lautrec!

FORGERIES OF AFFORDABLE ART

It is easier to fake pictures worth thousands rather than millions, because expensive pictures are examined more carefully. For example, affordable Russian art is booming, but so is the market in frauds as a result, and a flood of Russian fakes has been crossing the Swedish border. Recently Sotheby's were very excited to offer for sale a painting by Russian realist Ivan Shishkin, valued by them at £700,000 ($1,260,000). However, other experts believed it to be a doctored painting by an obscure Dutchman, Marinus Koekkoek, and as such probably worth less than £5,000 ($9,000). Indeed it was found that figures originally in the landscape had been removed and a signature inserted where before there was none. Russian experts believe that a number of ordinary Dutch paintings have been imported into Russia, been made to look like works by a Russian Master, then sent back to the West via Sweden. If you are interested in this area, always buy Russian art from a very respected art dealer, or research a piece at the Grabar Institute of Moscow. Because they see a lot of Russian art, the Bukowski auction house in Stockholm is also a good place to buy Russian works. (*See* Useful Contacts & Reference, pp.111 and 141.)

HOW TO MINIMIZE THE CHANCE OF BUYING A FAKE

Unfortunately, the more sophisticated fake-detection technology gets, the more devious forgers become. For instance, a small pocket ultraviolet torch can reveal a signature added on top of the varnish, so to combat this forgers varnish over the added signature. However, there are some things you can do to check the authenticity of a piece.

Good light Always view a picture in good light where you can see the texture of the paint better. When doing this you may be able to detect overpainting, or you may discover that the forger has used a different type or blend of paint, which was not available at the time when the original work was executed. A low-tech torch can help you examine the paint closely. A magnifying glass is also useful – one 13cm (5in) in diameter is strong enough to allow a generous viewing area.

Style If a work is atypical and inconsistent with the artist's usual work you should be wary. Art dealer Rupert Maas from London was initially taken in by the forged John Anster Fitzgeralds (see p.131), but felt that the colours were too hot on the pictures he was offered. He also added that the fairies' faces were simply wrong – "fakes done in the 1940s and 1950s have something of the Rita Hayworth… these have something contemporary and late 1990s about them." This latter point reminds us that fakes may take on the character of the time in which they were executed, so they can vary among themselves as well as in comparison with the original.

Materials There are certain things to look for, depending on the particular type of art you are looking at. For instance, acrylic paint was not invented in Victorian times, so a picture with a thick, matt, acrylic-like surface that purports to be 19th-century or earlier cannot be genuine.

Any watercolour on a single sheet of paper larger than 135 x 79cm (53 x 31in) must have been painted after 1772. Before that date it was impossible to produce a sheet of paper larger than this, but an invention in that year by James Whatman (comprising a system of frames and pulleys) enabled larger pieces to be made.

Early watercolours were also painted on laid paper, so-called because its components, soaked rags and cloths, were laid on parallel wires, which left an imprint or watermark lines on the wet paper. Whatman pioneered woven paper in the mid-18th century, replacing the parallel wires with wire mesh, which gave greater support and produced less obvious lines and a smoother surface. So, the more obvious the watermark, the older the watercolour or drawing.

Posters are always printed on low-quality paper and with sparing use of ink, so beware of a Toulouse Lautrec on well-printed or expensive-looking paper.

In the case of sculpture, original cast sculpture is taken from a resin or wax mould and the detail should be sharp and clear. When a piece is cast from another bronze, the definition of the animal's or person's hair, for example, is much less precise. Be aware that it is extremely difficult to tell if a bronze is a fake. Often even dealers with specialist knowledge and auction houses cannot tell, so if you are in any doubt, do not buy. Also, dates should correspond with history. If you see a work purporting to be made by a process invented after the suggested date of the work then you know you have a fake.

Provenance You should always seek provenance, which will help confirm that what you have is the genuine article, and also whether or not it is being sold legally. This is particularly true of sculpture and artifacts from the Middle East. There may not be a continuous line of ownership, but the proof of ownership should precede the Afghan and Iraq wars. Much illegal looting has gone on unchecked in these countries, which are treasure troves of Islamic and Buddhist artifacts. Laws surrounding exports are strict, and all countries with ancient civilizations take a very dim view of illegally exported works of art. (*See* chapter eight, Art & the Law, p.157.)

SIGNATURES

There are many stories about 20th-century artists and their profligacy with signatures. Salvador Dali signed bits of paper for money, Picasso doodled on restaurant bills to avoid paying, and when art historian Irving Sandler brushed up against a wet canvas in the late 1950s, the artist, whose name Sandler will not disclose, said he would not pay the cleaning bill but that perhaps the critic would like to bring over his jacket and he would sign it.

A signature does not always add value to a work. Some artists never signed their work, and if you see a signature on their paintings you should be suspicious. It is worth researching who signed their work and who did not, as some fraudsters may add signatures in the mistaken belief that that it adds value and authenticity. There are various books, such as the *The Visual Index of Artists' Signatures and Monograms,* that illustrate artists' signatures and stamps (*see* Useful Contacts & Reference, p.141).

HOW IMPORTANT ARE LETTERS AFTER AN ARTIST'S NAME?

Many artists we respect today rebelled against the academies of art, and therefore would not have had any letters after their names. The Impressionists are the most obvious example. Indeed, taking part in a controversial exhibition showcasing revolutionary art tends to enhance the artist's status as a rebel and outsider, and to increase the desirabillity of their work, at least in the longrun. To have shown in Paris at the Salon de Refusés, for example, is very important – these were artists, including Manet and Whistler, who were rejected by the committee for the official Salon. At the time people came in their droves to ridicule, but in the end they have stood the test of time and been accepted as masters. Equally, the Armory Show in New York in 1913 is claimed by *Who's Who in American Art* (*see* p.91) to have been the most important and influential exhibition of modern art in America. Americans flocked to see Europeans such as Picasso, Van Gogh, Braque, and Matisse, as well as their native Childe Hassam, John Sloan, Arthur Carles, and Joseph Stella. To have shown at the London exhibition *Sensation* in 1997, which made Damien Hirst and Tracey Emin internationally famous, also adds value to the work of all the exhibitors.

In more affordable fields, recognition by an artists' trade organization does add value, however. An artist must be elected by a panel of existing members, so a certain level of quality can be expected. Below are the initials of some societies that you may find after an artist's name. The prefix "Royal" can apply to British and Canadian organizations. To distinguish between the two "RCA"s you need to consider the context and nationality of the artist.

AAAA	American Association of Allied Arts
AFAS	American Fine Art Sociey
AWS	American Watercolor Society
BWS	British Watercolour Society
Calif AC	Californian Art Club
FRSA	Fellow of the Royal Society of Arts (UK)
IS	International Society of Sculptors, Painters, & Gravers
NAD	National Academy of Design (New York; since 1990 it has been the National Academy and School of Fine Arts)
NAWA	National Association of Women Artists (USA)
OSA	Ontario Society of Artists
PS	Pastel Society (UK or Canada; assoc. with Société des Pastellistes de France)
RA	Royal Academy (UK)
RBA	Royal Society of British Artists
RBS	Royal Society of British Sculptors
RCA	Royal Canadian Academy of Arts
RCA	Royal College of Art (UK)
RE	Royal Society of Etchers and Engravers (UK)
RHA	Royal Hibernian Academy (Ireland)
RIA	Royal Irish Academy
ROI	Royal Institute of Oil Painters (UK)
RP	Royal Institute of Portrait Painters (UK)
RSA	Royal Scottish Academy
RUA	Royal Ulster Academy of Arts
RSW	Royal Scottish Watercolour Society
RWS	Royal Watercolour Society (formerly Royal Society of Painters in Watercolours) (UK)
WCSI	Watercolour Society of Ireland

FRAUDULENT ART DEALERS

The most notorious dishonest art dealer of recent times is New Yorker Todd Volpe, who sold fakes to Hollywood stars including Jack Nicholson and Richard Gere, singer Barry Manilow, and clothes designer Calvin Klein. Like Myatt he started honestly, selling American Mission-style furniture and pictures in New York's Greenwich Village. It was how he presented and sold these items to his buyers that enticed fashionable New Yorkers. They loved what he sold, and he turned pieces that were once thought of as junk into valuable works of art. He then became an art advisor and was given money to buy pictures by the rich and famous. The problem was that he was starting to live like his rich clients, and could not always make enough on the pictures to support his lifestyle. He took their money and spent it on himself rather than buying a picture. He sold some of Jack Nicholson's pictures and did not pay him.

As the creditors closed in, he devised more elaborate schemes. He told a client that he could sell a picture for millions for which the client had paid a mere $10,000 (£6,250), but to do so the client had to make over the title of ownership to him. Volpe persuaded another investor that a picture was worth millions and that if he wanted to share in the profits he would have to invest $400,000 (£250,000) in it. The dealer agreed and Volpe gained $400,000 without ever owning the picture. Caught, and convicted in 1997, after his clients had decided to check what had happened to their money, Volpe has written a book called *Framed*, which is going to be turned into a film about the dirty dealings of the art world. *See* chapter five (p.115) for ways of finding a good dealer, and always remember to do your research and not blindly trust everything a dealer tells you.

BUYERS' TIP

Volpe's own tips for avoiding being duped are to look at a piece carefully and not to be over-impressed by glossy catalogues and florid descriptions.

ONLINE FRAUD

According to eBay there is very little fraud and deception on the Internet, affecting less than one hundreth of one per cent of total purchases. Nevertheless, all the listings cannot be monitored because there are so many, so, in order to help others, always report anything suspicious. In general, just be aware of the drawbacks of computer technology – there will always be risks posed by the unscrupulous minority.

Sniping One problem presented by this technology is known as sniping (a computer-programmed bid in the last second before closure, so beating the last highest bid). This may not be fraud or deception, but it is highly unfair and frustrating.

Fishing When you open your account you sign in over a secure site, but beware of emails sent to you asking for your password and identity. This process, known as fishing, involves crooks sending fake emails to online auction customers to obtain their details, which are then used to make purchases.

"Image hijacking" Another popular fraud involves copying someone else's photo of a work of art and "selling" it as the fraudster's own. The object has already been sold, however, so when you send in your money in good faith the artwork does not appear. Make sure when you buy that the picture and description are first class. A blurred picture with a scanty description is suspect. As you cannot see the piece you have no idea if its merits are being exaggerated

Credit card theft Credit card misappropriation is a concern for online auctions too. Cards are stolen and the numbers and other personal information used to take over dormant eBay profiles.

Fraudulent ratings eBay has a feedback system enabling you to rate buyers or sellers and read people's ratings before dealing with them. This system can be exploited of course. The company recently discovered a network of 30 dealers who had been providing exaggerated feedback for their friends' and colleagues' stock to increase each other's respectability.

Fortunately online auctioneers are responding to these problems and are setting fraud detection systems in place. eBay does have a list of possible fraudsters whom they monitor, and they use a behaviour pattern monitoring system, similar to a program used by credit card companies, which alerts them to any unusual spending patterns. They are also recruiting more staff to focus on honesty issues. Specialist online art and antiques auctioneer iGavel claims to screen all buyers and sellers who want to use their site, and they have a strict code of conduct to which sellers must sign up. They say that most of their sellers are professionals with whom they have had longstanding business relationships, and who guarantee the authenticity of the objects they sell. To combat sniping, Internet auctioneers are extending bidding time by an additional five minutes when it occurs.

HOW TO SAFEGUARD YOURSELF AGAINST POSSIBLE ONLINE FRAUD

Request photos Do not be afraid to ask the seller for further photographs – a keen and honest seller should be very willing to accommodate your request. Someone who electronically hijacks someone else's picture cannot provide a multitude of images or information because they do not own the actual work of art; they have just stolen its image.

Check addresses Ask the seller where the merchandise will be shipped from and where he or she lives. If the two differ ask for a reason for this.

Use safe payment methods Avoid transfers of cash, as if anything goes wrong they cannot be traced. It is best to use a method like eBay's PayPal buyer protection scheme, where you safeguard your credit card details by not giving them directly to the seller but through a secure site, or a cashier's cheque. Sellers of higher price items should accept escrow, where the buyer and seller agree to the terms and details of the transaction, and the buyer sends payment to a trusted third party such as www.escrow.com. Payment is verified and deposited into a trust account, the seller ships the merchandise to the buyer, knowing that the buyer's payment is secured, the buyer accepts the merchandise after having the opportunity to inspect it, and finally escrow.com pays the seller after all the conditions of the transaction are met.

Check feedback If you become suspicious of a seller, or even as a matter of course, check the feedback on them. If you notice an unusually high level of feedback it might be artificial, but although vulnerable to abuse, the feedback system still remains a very useful tool for checking up on potential buyers or sellers.

Check consistency Professional art dealers on the net should continue to sell the same kind of items. If someone is advertising themselves as a professional, then ensure that previous transactions were in the same field. It is okay for a private person to sell a washing machine one week and a Picasso drawing another, but it is not usual for someone in the art business to do this kind of thing.

Keep records Most importantly, keep a record of every detail of your online transactions, because without documentation it will be impossible to prove fraudulent behaviour. Report any vendor you think is behaving suspiciously. Fraud is a criminal offence and if you feel strongly you could pursue the matter through the courts.

BUYERS' TIP

Although online auctioneers try very hard to combat and eradicate fraudulent dealings, they will not pay compensation. *Caveat emptor*, or "buyer beware", is the maxim to adopt.

USEFUL CONTACTS & REFERENCE

RUSSIAN ART FORGERY

Grabar Institute of Moscow The Grabar Institute will be able to advise you on Russian artists and their styles, which should help arm you with the knowledge to avoid fakes. Visit the Grabar Art Conservation Centre at 60/2, Bol.Ordynka str., Moscow, Russia. Tel: (095) 951-02-84; e-mail: grabar@sovintel.ru.

SIGNATURE REFERENCE WORKS

Useful for researching when to expect a signature and when not, and what they should look like.

Artists as Illustrators: An International Directory with Signatures and Monograms, 1800–Present More than 14,000 entries of 19th- and 20th-century artists. Entries include illustrators, sculptors, and fine art artists. (John Castagno, Scarecrow Press, 1989)

Artists' Monograms and Indiscernible Signatures: An International Directory, 1800–1991 A very useful work by John Castagno, including 5,200 signatures of 3,700 artists worldwide, listing nationality, birth and death dates, and reference sources. (Scarecrow Press, New Jersey and London, 1991)

The Visual Index of Artists' Signatures and Monograms Presents alphabetically facsimiles of the signatures of European painters who flourished between the 15th century and the present. (Radway Jackson, Alpine Fine Arts Collection, 1991)

Who Was Who in American Art and *Who's Who in American Art* These works contain the signatures of American artists, and more (*see* p.91 for details).

BECOMING A COLLECTOR

"Those who truly love art will buy regardless of the hype or the lack of it." Rome Jorge, *The Manila Times*

What you will learn in this chapter:

• What you need to be a successful collector

• Trends and ways of collecting

• Advice on opening an art gallery

Firstly, think about why you want to collect art (as opposed to buy the odd piece): is it primarily for personal pleasure or for long-term investment? Do you want to buy and sell regularly? If it is for investment and profit, you have to accept that a true appreciation of the art you are buying must still come first. The best art collections are formed with passion and not with an eye to profit. The best collectors are prepared to take risks and go to any lengths, short of theft and murder, to find what they want. The thrill of the hunt should have a strong appeal.

A successful collection is personal: it expresses the character

> **BUYERS' TIP**
> The greatest collections are not amassed for profit. The collectors may be rich but they thrive on taking risks, which is how they become rich. Investing in art therefore appeals to them.

of the collector. He or she can find idiosyncrasies in the work of artists that might not appeal to everyone, yet make the work more interesting in the long run. It may be helpful to draw inspiration from other perceptive collectors.

NOTABLE COLLECTORS

One collector that stands out is Peggy Guggenheim. This scion of the famous art-collecting family, whose palazzo in Venice is well worth a visit, collected art in a rather individual way. She was rich, but it was not just through her wealth that she acquired work by some of the most important mid-20th-century artists, such as Magritte, Max Ernst, Kandinsky, Chagall, Modigliani, Jackson Pollock, and many others, all before they were famous. She had three important qualities: good taste, discernment, and a willingness to take risks. An eccentric character, she dressed outrageously and always had her dogs in tow. Artists sold her their most experimental and uncommercial work, so her Venice home, which is now a museum, contains works by famous artists the likes of which you do not see in other museums. These are now extremely valuable. Just as there are stories of French Impressionists swapping artworks for food and drink with café owners, so Peggy became part of the artists' lives, pampering their egos, collecting medicine for them, and generally making herself indispensable. When the elderly Piet Mondrian walked into her London gallery, Guggenheim Jeune, rather than talk about art she took him on a tour of dance halls. She had relationships with artists from Marcel Duchamp to Yves Tanguy and, indeed, she married Max Ernst. When Tanguy's wife found out about the affair she threw a plate of fish over Peggy when she saw her eating in the same restaurant.

A mandatory visit in Britain for the budding art collector should be to Kettle's Yard in Cambridge, the home of H.S. "Jim" and Helen Ede, now open to the public. The couple, who were distinctly less wealthy than Peggy Guggenheim, collected British mid-20th-century art, and Jim was also a curator and writer on art. He became a friend and supporter of young aspiring artists, including the then-unknown Ben Nicholson, whom he met when the latter was buying work by the Cornish fisherman Alfred Wallis, now a highly collected artist. Both are represented at Kettle's Yard. Ede also rescued the estate of the sculptor Henri Gaudier-Brzeska, whose works he found dumped in the boardroom at the Tate, having been deemed unsuitable for inclusion in the museum.

The Edes' greatest triumph was to display and show off artworks to their best effect. The pieces did not stand in sterile isolation, but became part of the fabric of the couple's lives. Sketches, prints, painting, and sculpture were not collected merely as trophies. A Ben Nicholson linocut would be propped up against an electric socket, a Gaudier-Brzeska sculpture placed next to a cracked plate. This intermingling of furniture, glass, and natural objects still reigns at Kettle's Yard; everywhere are objects from nature, pebbles and seed pods in among the artworks, retaining Jim's vision of "simply a collection of works of art reflecting my taste or the taste of a given period".

BUYERS' TIP

Collecting contemporary art can be exciting. You can take a gamble on a relatively cheap picture by an unknown artist whose work might one day turn out to be very valuable. But as with any form of gambling, never spend money that you cannot afford to lose.

COLLECTING TRENDS

The economic boom of the late 1990s made a number of young people very rich, both in the United States and across Europe. According to New York dealers, these people are extremely well informed – with an enthusiasm veering on the obsessive – and mix socially in the art scene. They are mostly aged between 35 and 45, and Will Ameringer of Ameringer and Yohe Fine Art in

New York says that as much as 20 per cent of his sales come from this group today, more than double the percentage of the previous five years.

These young collectors buy contemporary work by artists of their own generation, and have done their research into who is hot. They not only scour locally, but also search the Internet for catalogues from galleries all over the United States and Europe. These collectors are not satisfied with a picture that is merely good; they want the best.

Past generations often collected in certain specialist areas – English 18th-century watercolours or American folk art, for example. The advantage of this is that it is easier to become an expert in a narrow field, to notice things that perhaps others do not, and therefore to get good deals. It also means, perhaps with less narrowly specific areas, that you can theme your surroundings to suit your favoured area of art, to create a satisfyingly "complete" environment. For example, you may collect 1960s and 70s Pop and Op art, so you would fill your home with all things from the era – furniture, lighting, kitchenalia, and so on, in an appropriately period-style setting. You might even buy and wear vintage clothing of the era.

Nowadays, however, many collectors do not warm to this restrictive, and potentially obsessive, method of collecting, where you are effectively trying to re-create another place and time. Instead they have more eclectic tastes, mixing artists from different periods and countries. Contemporary interior design taste also actively encourages this approach. A good dealer whom you can trust is therefore a great help if you are collecting in a wide area.

Naturally art dealers are currently cultivating these new buyers, and galleries are organizing private parties to entertain them. Museums, too, are responding with young collectors' groups. Of course there have always been friends' and associates' groups for very rich prospective donors for the purchase of new work, but now there are clubs within most major museums in Europe and North America that will cater for those on a more modest budget. Museums around the world, such as the Museum of Modern Art in New York, organize social events, lecture trips, and studio visits. The Tate Gallery in London has a Patrons' Scheme, membership of which enables you to tour the galleries with curators, visit private collections and artists' studios, and attend special show openings where you can meet artists, writers, and others with a specialized knowledge of art.

SO WHAT ARE THE ESSENTIAL QUALITIES FOR A COLLECTOR?

Passion You must take pleasure from art and be committed to expending energy in proportion to what you seek to gain from it.

Knowledge As we have seen, it is imperative to go out actively and learn the basics of art history, and to discover where your interests lie, whom you like, and what is happening in the art world. Never stop absorbing information.

Good taste and discernment This is something almost innate, but good judgment can be refined by experience and knowledge.

Confidence Learn to trust your eyes and your instinct, rather than follow the crowd.

Willingness to take risks Sometimes you just have to take the plunge if you want to be pleasantly surprised, but try to retain a degree of calculation in your risk-taking.

OPENING YOUR OWN ART GALLERY: A CASE STUDY

If collecting takes over your life, there is always a temptation to give up your boring day job and to make work "enjoyable". Many of us dream of escaping from the city and moving to a small town or village. However, although rents may be cheap, starting a gallery in a rural area could be very risky.

Sixteen years ago Christopher and Deborah Harrison decided to open an art gallery – a brave move because they could not afford a premises in a picturesque tourist town. Their budget stretched only to an outbuilding attached to their tiny cottage in a remote English village. "We felt as if we were real pioneers," Christopher recalls. "We were selling work by contemporary artists and the local taste was for Victorian watercolours and traditional rural landscapes." But the gallery had to work, as they were going to depend on it for their income: it was not just a hobby. Christopher and Deborah took out a bank loan for renovation work to the outbuilding and set to work creating the Bircham Gallery in Norfolk. Today the Bircham Gallery is located in larger premises in Holt, a Norfolk town that is popular with tourists, and employs four people.

THE ROUTE TO SUCCESS

Publicity and contacts "We had to make our presence known so we did a lot of publicity. The arts centre in the larger town nearby gave us their mailing list. We had postcards made of some of the artists we wanted to sell, and wrote to many people," says Christopher. Luckily an important and influential local figure responded very enthusiastically and brought friends along to their first exhibition. So many businesses succeed through word of mouth: if a well-respected figure gives an art gallery their approval, others will follow.

Representative The Harrisons felt that the artists and sculptors they showed should have a connection with the local area. "We chose artists who we feel still have something to say, and although not all paint Norfolk scenes, 50 per cent do." The Bircham Gallery wanted to offer interesting alternatives to the typical quaint figurative watercolour. Luckily enough people supported their aims, and exhibitions at the gallery started to sell out.

Quality and affordabillity The Harrisons built up a reputation for high-quality, low-cost art, to the extent that people would make special pilgrimages to their gallery. Their most expensive exhibits are around £5,000 ($9,000) for work by a world-famous artist, a rare Henry Moore print for example. At the other end of the spectrum they sell etchings by young artists for just £20 ($36).

Merchandising They decided to sell postcards, art magazines, and small linocuts and craft, so that most customers would be able to buy something.

Stock They have about six exhibitions a year and have a permanent stock of the work of 25 painters and 100 printmakers. This means that customers who have seen exhibitions in the past and liked the artists, but for one reason or another have not bought at the time, can view more of the artists' work.

Integrity On average, Christopher and Deborah get three letters or visits a week from artists wanting to show at the gallery. "We are very definite about what we like and will not be deflected. We will not show work purely because we think it will sell, it has to have an artistic integrity we believe in." Christopher feels that in the beginning he was far too keen to take on artists without seeing the body of their work. On later finding inconsistencies of quality, he found it rather embarrassing to disengage from them.

THE BUSINESS SIDE

The Harrrisons stress that they are not art dealers. They do not buy and sell art, but rather take work on consignment. Artists are invited to show at the Bircham Gallery. The artist pays for framing; the gallery sends out invitations from their mailing list and mounts the exhibition, with a private view for valued clients. The gallery takes 40 per cent of a picture's selling price, and can cautiously increase prices of very popular artists when demand exceeds supply. The gallery is not the sole representative of any artist, but it does have an exclusivity zone of a 100-mile radius.

They were sponsored by a rural development agency to do a basic business course, but feel that an in-depth business background is not essential when founding an art gallery. They both come from arts disciplines, and are grateful that they can evaluate and discuss the aesthetics of an artist's output.

USEFUL CONTACTS & REFERENCE

LEARNING AND NETWORKING

Auction houses Auction houses such as Christie's and Sotheby's do fine art courses that can help a budding collector gain the background knowledge so essential in art collecting: *see* p.32.

Kettle's Yard The Edes' old home-cum-art space in Cambridge is open throughout the year and also runs free lectures – well worth a visit. Go to www.kettlesyard.co.uk or call +44 (0)1223 352 124.

Museum of Modern Art The big New York museum of modern art organizes social events, courses, lecture trips, and studio visits. Visit www.moma.org or call +1 212 708 9781.

Museums in the USA This is a very comprehensive online database that lists all American museums by state or by specialist area. It is free to access, and might help the collector find a museum specializing in his or her interest. The museums can also be contacted in relation to membership and courses. Visit www.museumca.org/usa.

Peggy Guggenheim Collection It is definitely worth making a trip to Venice to see Peggy's stunning collection at the Palazzo Venier dei Leoni. Visit www.guggenheim-venice.it or call +39 041 2405 411.

Tate Gallery This London group of galleries has a wide range of programmes to suit collectors of all budgets. Visit www.tate.org.uk or see the Directory starting on p.183 for other museums and galleries.

OPENING A GALLERY

Bircham Gallery The Harrisons' gallery in Norfolk. Visit www.bircham-arts.co.uk or call +44 (0)1263 713312.

Department of Trade and Industry This UK government body can advise on starting a new business, including an art gallery. It is best to phone Business Link to find out more about who to talk to in your area. Visit www.businesslink.gov.uk or www.dti.gov.uk, or call Business Link on +44 (0)845 600 9006.

ART & THE LAW

"... the strangest realisation... is that it isn't so much that fame attracts thieves as that thieves, floods, fires, and wars create fame."
Jonathan Jones, *The Guardian*

What you will learn in this chapter:

- How to go about insuring your works of art
- What taxes you may or may not have to pay when inheriting works of art
- The rules behind exporting and importing art
- What to do if you suspect you may have inadvertently bought stolen artwork, or if you are the victim of theft

Although Jonathan Jones makes an acutely observed point – that the theft or loss of art can in fact create an aura of publicity and fame that stokes the work's mystery and power – in reality this is not likely to be the result of the loss of your own artwork, and of course it will never be your aim when buying a piece. Imagine the upset and disappointment if the beautiful painting or sculpture that you carefully researched and bought at such a good price is stolen, or turns out to be stolen property and you have to return it. Or imagine that your favourite picture was damaged in transit and it was not even properly insured. In order to avoid risking such disappointment, you must ensure you have all the facts and protect yourself as much as possible against all eventualities.

The most common types of damage stated in insurance claims

are those caused by smoke, water, or breakage during transit. Sometimes works of art are stolen. The most common method of art theft is known in police circles as "photographic", in which a thief breaks in and mysteriously does not steal anything. Do not think that you have seen the last of them, however. In a photographic crime a robber breaks in and photographs any interesting artwork; when he finds someone interested in a specific piece he then returns and removes it to order.

The wars in Afghanistan and Iraq have seen an increase in the number of works of art being smuggled out of these countries illegally. Possession of one of these smuggled pieces could land the person receiving them in serious trouble. These are very rare but real possibilities, and there are ways of being prepared for them. This chapter deals with some of the legal, tax, and insurance aspects of owning original artworks.

INSURING YOUR ART

If you have more than £5,000 ($9,000) worth of art in your home you may well be able to save money by insuring through a specialist company. With the growth in art purchases over recent years, insurance companies have risen to the increased demand and are competing among themselves to insure fine art. A number of companies specialize in this field – Axa Nordstern and Chubb worldwide, and Hiscox in London are three of the best.

Generally, insurance valuations reflect the cost of replacement, but when you damage a picture or sculpture you cannot just go out and buy another piece that is exactly the same. This is why specialist insurance agents are appropriate, as they can recommend a good restorer. (*See* Useful Contacts & Reference, p.159.)

It is vital that you insure any pieces of art in your possession, even if they are on loan. In the latter case it is a good idea to check with the owner to see whether their insurance is valid outside their home. If you are transporting a work of art via air or truck, make sure that the carrier's insurance covers the full value of your art. All carriers have insurance, but it is worth checking that it is sufficient.

Different insurance companies will have different requirements. However, most non-specialist ones say that any individual item worth over £1,000 ($1,800) should be listed individually on your insurance cover documents.

It is a good idea to photograph your artworks carefully both from the front and back and keep the photographs safe. Note the dimensions of the pieces too. Keep all purchase, restoration, and framing receipts, and descriptions as well. This will make things easier if you ever need to make a claim.

VALUATION & APPRAISAL FOR INSURANCE & PROBATE

Most auction houses will appraise your art for insurance purposes. Their charges used to be calculated on a percentage basis, but now everyone charges an hourly or daily rate.

However, when using auction houses be aware of their agenda. Valuation for them is a sideline, and they are really in business to buy and sell. Of course they will do an honest and good job, but it has been known for an auctioneer to value low in order to reduce the risk of disappointment and accusations, should you decide to sell and the piece does not fetch its true worth. A client will be pleasantly surprised if something goes for a higher price than they were expecting, but not if it goes for a lower one. Auction estimates are the trade valuation.

When someone dies, a solicitor will arrange a valuation of their property for what is known as probate (the providing of wills and dealing with deceased clients' estates). These probate valuations are needed to work out inheritance tax (see p.153), and are often on the low side because descendants want to pay as little as they can.

Specialist insurance valuers, such as Gurr Johns in London

and New York, will send a specialist to view the pieces, or a number of specialists in different fields if your collection is diverse. Find out how much they charge first, and give a clear description of what is in the house so that the right person will come and visit. You do not want to waste your time and money!

> **BE AWARE**
> If you own a piece that an auction house really wants to sell, they
> may continue to pester you to give it to them for sale.

INHERITANCE & CAPITAL GAINS TAX

When a relative leaves you a fairly valuable piece of art in their will you will probably have to pay inheritance tax, unless it is from your spouse. Generally, in the UK, gifts made to individuals more than seven years before your death, such as money and possessions made over to a child, will not incur inheritance tax when you die. However, governments are keen to plug loopholes and laws change all the time, so it is always best to check details with an accountant or solicitor.

If a work of art is what the Inland Revenue calls a pre-eminent asset, then no tax is payable. A pre-eminent asset is not necessarily a very valuable one, but something unusual and of historic and cultural interest to the country. For example, a portrait of Jane Austen, important because of the subject matter, might be considered to be pre-eminent. For a work to qualify for the tax exemption, the public must have access to it for a month each year. If you did not want people tramping through your home then a museum loan would suffice.

If you make a gift of an artwork to another person or a company or trust, you will be treated as if you had sold the asset at its market value and may have to pay capital gains tax. This will be charged on any increase in the value of the asset since you acquired it. The taxable profit is assessed on a 1982 valuation plus an annual price growth figure. If the value exceeds the agreed annual growth figure then you pay tax on the difference between the two. A gift you make to your husband or wife when you are living together is not normally liable to capital gains tax.

Aside from it being hard to digest, space does not permit me to go through the tax laws for every country in the world. Each country has different rules, but, generally speaking, authorities do not like good works of art to leave the country, so tax breaks in most countries are available for museum donations in order to encourage the keeping of the art in its native country.

MUSEUM DONATIONS

Many collections, not just those of high value, are dispersed or given to a museum after the owner's death. There are different reasons for this. The collector may wish others to appreciate his or her life's work and therefore gives instruction for a museum to be opened, provided of course they have left sufficient funds to run it. Alternatively, the collector's relatives might have different tastes and so prefer to sell the pieces. Sadly, if the collector has not made wise tax provisions the relatives may have to sell or donate pieces to pay death duties.

Some collectors also choose to arrange for their artworks to be given or lent on long lease to a museum or other charitable organization on their death, in order to save their relatives from having to pay inheritance tax. Whatever the reason, the museum or gallery has to want the piece in the first place: you cannot expect a museum to accept pictures or sculpture automatically, as their storerooms are probably already groaning with work that they cannot display for lack of space.

In the United States, Congress passed a law over 20 years ago permitting art collections, no matter how valuable, to pass between spouses on the death of one without any tax being due. In addition, if, as a United States citizen, you donate something to another family member in your lifetime rather than after death, you could still pay considerably less tax. Again, as mentioned above with regard to inheritance in the UK, it is advisable to talk to a professional, as tax law changes frequently.

The United States taxation system has given favourable recognition to charitable donations of works of art for a long time. They will allow a donor to carry forward his or her tax-deductible gift allowances over five years. This means that if you want to make a donation to a museum or a private collection recognized as a charity but find that the fair market value of the art is greater than the amount you wish to give, you may give a percentage of the artwork. This means that you and the charity share ownership. For example, if 50 per cent of a sculpture is given to charity, the original owner and the charity can each have it for half the year and benefit from the tax breaks available.

EXPORT LICENCES & IMPORT DUTIES

Export licensing controls for objects of cultural interest are necessary to balance the need to keep nationally important objects in a country, the rights of owners, and the stimulation of a healthy national art trade. In the UK, all cultural objects – paintings, sculpture, pottery, or any handmade works that represent the culture of the nation, and are over 50 years old and above a certain value – need an export licence to leave the country. Thresholds vary wildly, however: an oil painting has to be worth over £91,000 ($164,000) to need one, whereas a photograph has to be worth only £10,000 ($18,000). Even objects under 50 years old cannot be exported without a licence if they are of particular cultural importance.

Free UK export licences used to be available from the Department for Culture, Media, and Sport. The department can still furnish you with further information, but since May 2005 licensing has been dealt with by the Museums, Libraries, and Archives Council (MLA), where it has become part of the MLA's Acquisition, Export, and Loans Unit (see Useful Contacts & Reference, p.160).

Export licences are not required for objects leaving the United

States, but when importing works of art from Europe and Asia into the USA an authentic export licence from the country of origin is required. At the time of writing no customs or import duty is owed to the American authorities for original works of art. This term includes paintings, as well as prints produced by hand from handmade originals, and the first 12 castings of an original sculpture. A reproduction of a print, poster, or photograph printed today and made in large quantities would be liable for local import duty if the poster exceeded the amount of goods you are allowed to bring in to the country tax free.

A NATION KEEPS ITS HERITAGE

Recently a British family offered a cache of important Victorian photographs for sale at auction. Just before the sale the Museum of Photography stepped in and argued that the photographs should be kept within the UK because they were of national importance. The museum then applied to the government to defer the granting of an export licence for six months (the museum could have asked for three months or a year), to give them time to match what was paid on the hammer. The seller can refuse this offer, but if no export licence is granted they cannot let the object leave the country, whatever price a buyer is prepared to pay. The happy outcome of this situation is that the purchaser of the photographs has lent them to a British museum. As an American citizen he gets a tax break for this, but he still owns the photographs.

IMPORT DUTY & SALES TAX

An import duty of five per cent VAT (Value Added Tax) is due on pieces entering the UK from outside the EU, regardless of age, if they are deemed works of art by Customs and Excise. This duty varies up to ten per cent in other EU countries. When you import from within the EU no import duty is payable. Auction houses and dealers collect this tax from the buyer and pay it. If you buy at auction you also have to pay the standard 17.5 per cent VAT on the auctioneer's commission. If you are exporting to the United States, however, you can claim back the European sales taxes of five per cent and pay local state sales tax, which varies between individual states. You may also have to pay an import duty, known as MPS, of 0.21 per cent of the value of the item if it is worth more than $480 (£270).

All the auction houses have an export department, so to avoid paying local sales tax on the sales commission, get a form from them to produce at customs, which will waive tax. A number of carriers, such as Gander and White, and Cadogan Tate, will organize all this paperwork. Art dealers will also furnish you with it or tell you where to acquire the form.

LOOTED TREASURES

Obviously, purchasing an ancient Greek head without provenance is unwise for two reasons. It might be a fake, or alternatively it might have been stolen from a poor or war-torn country and exported without a proper export licence. Countries such as Turkey and Greece come down very harshly on theft from ancient sites. When a country is as unstable as Iraq or Afghanistan, moreover, the opportunities for looting are great. Fortunately, initial estimates of losses from the Iraq National Museum were far higher than is now believed to be the case, and many objects were discovered in a place of safety. But there are still some 3,000 items missing from this very important museum, and the British and American governments are working closely with the new Iraqi government to recover these objects.

WHAT TO DO IF YOU ARE IN THE POSSESSION OF STOLEN ARTWORK

If you have bought in good faith a little bronze figure thought to be Persian and the police call and say that it has been stolen from a museum in Tehran, what do you do? The law differs from country to country. To generalize, most countries tend to favour the dispossessed rather than the *bona fide* purchaser, which means you would lose the piece and the money you paid for it, even if you bought it unwittingly. Ignorance is no excuse for receiving a stolen object.

Nevertheless, before you surrender the object ask them what the basis of their claim is. They should be able to offer substantial proof that the object in your possession is the exact object that has been stolen. The time when it left its country of origin is important because after a number of years (check with relevant government departments such as the Department of Culture, Media, and Sport in the UK for specific figures – *see* Useful Contacts & Reference, p.160), the government of the country no longer has title over the work of art.

If you suspect yourself that a piece you have just bought may in fact be a stolen work, then make sure you are armed with the facts. Go and read up on the artist so that you are very familiar with the work. Then if you are still suspicious call the police. You can match an image against the database of 70,000 pictures held by Trace, for example (*see* Useful Contacts & Reference, p.161).

Companies such as Withers, in London and New York, specialize in all aspects of the law relating to art and cultural property and can help, but of course they do not come cheap. Try to avoid a legal wrangle unless the object is very valuable. If you have unknowingly received looted goods then you will merely be asked to hand them back. It is the thieves and their accomplices who will be prosecuted under criminal law.

BUYERS' TIP

At the present time there are special laws surrounding objects from Iraq. Unless you can show that the object left Iraq before the first Gulf War then you are handling stolen goods. Be very careful when investing in a Mesopotamian object (Mesopotamia is now Iraq). The law in Britain at the moment is on the side of the Iraqis. You are presumed guilty of cultural theft unless you can prove otherwise.

WHAT TO DO IF YOUR ART IS STOLEN IN A BURGLARY

Obviously this is very distressing. Often the pieces you have lost may be irreplaceable and monetary compensation may be no consolation, but always make sure that you are insured properly so as to soften the blow should this eventuality occur (*see* Insuring Your Art, p.151). If your art is stolen, always report it to the police, giving them as much information as possible about when, where, and what, with full descriptions.

Though you may think it is a lost cause, there is always the possibility of retrieving your works via a service such as Trace. This is a tracking service for thefts in the UK and the rest of the world. When Trace is provided with details by the police of when and where a burglary took place, a police case number, photograph, and a brief description, the artwork is entered on their database. Their police team, which has art knowledge, liaises with forces worldwide to try and recover the stolen objects. They claim that recovery rates for pictures are high because they are easily identifiable, although it can take up to five years to get them back. Part of the explanation for this is that drug dealers sometimes steal pictures from museums or stately homes to be used as a form of collateral or insurance policy against someone not paying up – almost as if the museums or stately homes are banks from which they can withdraw pictures rather than banknotes, so to speak. The pictures are hidden until the debtor pays up, when they are released back onto the market. It costs £50 ($90) to be included on the database, and £125 ($225) for an eighth-page advertisement in *Trace Magazine.*

USEFUL CONTACTS & REFERENCE

INSURANCE AND VALUATION

Axa Nordstern This international art insurer has a very informative website, targeted at people beginning art collections. Visit www.axa-art.com or call in the UK on +44

(0)20 7265 4600 or in the United States on +1 877 AXA 4 ART.
Chubb Chubb have offices worldwide and offer competitive
insurance policies for fine art. Visit the personal insurance and
fine art sections of www.chubb.com or call in the UK on +44
(0)20 7956 5000 or in the United States on +1 866 324 8222.
Gurr Johns A well-established art valuation and consultancy
firm independent of auctioneers or dealers, with offices in
London, New York, Paris, and Munich. Visit www.gurrjohns.com
or call in the UK on +44 (0)20 7839 4747 or in the United
States on +1 212 486 7373.
Hiscox An efficient and knowledgeable insurance company
who have insured works of art for many years. You can even
get quotes on line (the site is secure) for your art collection. Visit
www.hiscox.com or call in the UK on +44 (0)845 345 1666.

TAX, LICENCES, LAW
Cadogan Tate This international shipper of fine art and
antiques is one of a number who will sort all paperwork to do
with tax and duties (*see also* Gander and White below). Visit
www.cadogantate.com or call +44 (0) 20 7819 6600 in the UK
or +1 718 706 7999 in the United States.
Department of Culture, Media, and Sport This UK
government department can advise on any export issues, and on
illicit trade in antiquities. Visit www.culture.gov.uk/cultural_property.
The Museums, Libraries and Archives Council now provide
export licences, so visit their website at www.mla.gov.uk or call
+44 (0)20 7078 6280, and write to the following to apply for a
licence: Acquisition Export and Loans Unit, 3rd Floor 83 Victoria
Street, London SW1 OHW.
Gander and White An international shipper of fine art and
antiques able to handle all paperwork to do with tax and duties.
Visit www.ganderandwhite.com or call +44 (0)20 8971 7171 in
the UK or +1 718 784 8444 in the United States.
Her Majesty's Revenue and Customs This is the UK
government tax body (the old Inland Revenue and Customs and

Excise combined) and can help with all related questions. Visit
www.hmrc.gov.uk or call the Probate and Inheritance Tax
Helpline on +44 (0)845 3020 900.

Internal Revenue Service Part of the American Department
Of The Treasury, available for help with inheritance and capital
gains tax queries. Visit www.irs.gov or call +1 800 829 1040.

An Overview of Issues of Interest to the Art Collector
Written by lawyer Steven Thomas, this provides further
information on tax implications for American art collectors.
Phone Irell and Manella LLP on +1 310 277 1010 or order
from the website, www.irell.com.

Withers Among other areas, Withers specializes in the
law surrounding cultural objects, with offices in London and
New York. They are excellent but expensive to hire. Visit
www.withersworldwide.com or call in the UK on +44 (0)20
7597 6000 or in the United States on +1 212 848 9800.

THEFT TRACKING

The Art Loss Register Claims to be the world's largest private
international database of lost and stolen art, antiques, and
collectables. Visit www.artloss.com or call +44 (0)20 7928 0100
in the UK or +1 212 297 0941 in the United States.

Invaluable This independent service was set up to help bidders
find art from all over the world, but they also offer a facility that
alerts subscribers if their stolen art comes up for auction. Visit
www.invaluable.com, call customer services in the UK on 0800
376 8592, or call internationally on +44 (0)1983 281 155.

Object ID Helps to combat art theft by encouraging the
use of an international standard for describing art, antiques,
and antiquities. Visit www.object-id.com or call +44 (0)1747
841540.

Trace This service searches for stolen art, antiques, and
collectables and is open to anyone in the world. It also publishes
Trace Magazine. Visit www.trace.co.uk or call 0800 376 8592
within the UK and +44 (0)1983 281 155 outside the UK.

CARE & DISPLAY OF YOUR ART

"When something is of value to us we spend time with it, time enjoying it and time taking care of it." Jackson Pollock

What you will learn in this chapter:

- How to move and store works of art
- How to position and display your art
- How to light your artwork
- Pointers on cleaning and restoration

The care of your art may seem an obvious consideration, but it is surprising how easy it is to make an exciting acquisition that is fussed over and admired for some time, but soon becomes such a familiar fixture of the household that it blends in and is all but forgotten. Either way, whether your art is constantly in the spotlight or in a little-used corridor, it is vulnerable to damage through both over-eager handling and neglect. This chapter considers a few of the more pertinent points to remember.

MOVING & STORING WORKS OF ART

It is very easy, when caught up in the euphoria of art purchase, to try and get the piece home as soon as possible in the back of the car. Do not be impatient, however: works of art have to be transported and looked after with care. A damaged painting or sculpture is worth considerably less than it is in good condition. Here are a few things to consider when moving or storing art:

Wrapping When moving a sculpture from the studio or gallery, make sure that it is wrapped up in padding inside its box to avoid any movement. Make sure that no part protrudes over the edge of the box. Never lift a sculpture by its extremities, such as a limb, as they could break off. Always lift with two hands, one at the bottom and the other at the top of the piece. This ensures that you have the sculpture secure in case you trip. Obviously, never try and lift something by yourself if you are in any doubt about whether you can manage it.

Stacking When stacking pictures, make sure that you place them back-to-back to avoid damage to the glass or canvas. Put the largest picture against the wall with a foam board bigger than the external dimensions of the frame behind it. Alternatively, use a blanket at the front and back, or cover the pictures in bubble wrap then stack them in descending order of size. It is not advisable to stack more than five pictures against each other, as the combined pressure could damage the picture at the back of the pile.

Temperature Never store pictures or sculpture intended for the house in an outside barn or shed where the temperature could fall to below freezing point. Very low temperatures damage pictures and can crack some sculpture.

Water risks Never move anything with wet hands: water can damage some materials and, of course, objects might slip out of your hands and break.

Flaking paint If you find a picture with flaking paint that you just have to have, do not bring it into a centrally heated room. To slow down the flaking, store it on its side to help counter the natural direction of the falling paint, in a damp, dark place inside the house to minimize brittleness.

Frames If you are handling pictures with old gilt or soft matt frames, handle them while wearing white gloves, as perspiration or dirt from your hands could cause damage. Gilding is very susceptible to extremes of temperature and begins to flake if too hot, too cold, or too damp.

POSITIONING & DISPLAYING ART

The way we display art greatly affects the way it is perceived, interpreted, and enjoyed – and we all want to show off our pieces to their best advantage. When deciding where and how to hang or display them, there are some points to consider:

Light damage When hanging a new picture in any medium ensure that it is away from strong light, such as sunlight, particularly if it is a watercolour, which will fade very quickly.

Water damage Obviously avoid any risk of water getting near a piece (including condensation); do not hang it above a basin, bath, or anywhere where water might seep down from overflowing basins, and even radiators. Again, watercolours are particularly sensitive.

Heat damage Hanging a picture above a radiator is not a good idea, as the rising heat can crack the paint and canvas.

Humidity What pictures like best is relative humidity. If the level of humidity is above 50 per cent they are happy. Central heating is the usual cause of reduced humidity, but it is possible to buy a humidifier that counters its drying effect, and you can also buy portable machines that measure humidity (see Useful Contacts & Reference, pp.170–1).

Tactical positioning It may sound obvious, but do not put a sculpture in a place where it can be knocked over. Always consider whether it could be a trip hazard when shortlisting positions for it. Ensure treasured pictures are not hung in narrow corridors where they can easily be knocked, especially if you have children or pets who like to run between rooms.

Pedestals Make sure the pedestal you place your sculpture on is strong enough and in a contrasting material, so that it offsets the piece well. Perspex or wood look good with stone, for example.

Picture groups When hanging a "collage" of prints, photographs, small oils, and watercolours, it is a good idea to measure your layout on the floor first. Start with the central picture and work outwards. The amount of space between the pictures will depend on the size of the wall: you do not want pictures all crammed together on a long and high wall, but then on a large wall it often looks rather feeble to have many tiny pictures anyway. For a set of pictures of the same size it looks good to allow space between them that is the same width of one of the pictures. The edges of frames should always be neatly parallel with each other. There is nothing wrong with a collage of different shapes, sizes, and frames. It does not matter, either, if they are all in different media. But be wary of putting a slim frame next to a chunky one, or a heavy oil next to a delicate watercolour.

"If you are close to it, a big painting is just a feeling around you, that's all." James Rosenquist

Picture level Pictures should be hung at eye level. That is, average eye level – I find that many people hang pictures too high, in line with the eyes of a six-foot man. Pictures always look better hanging lower rather than higher, so think in terms of the eye level of a woman of average height; or simply consider the heights of the particular people who will be seeing the picture regularly. Larger pictures that are intended to be seen from a distance are an exception, and can sometimes work better higher up.

FRAMING A PICTURE

An appropriate frame will enhance a picture, not overpower it. Framing tastes change, and nowadays we are less keen on gilt frames and all the attached curlicues. Modern oils look good in a simple wooden frame. I saw an 18th-century picture of a pair of greyhounds framed in a simple silver frame, which looked very smart with hints of silvery grey in the dogs' coats reflected in the frame. Whatever your tastes, there are some practical points to consider when framing:

Watercolours Many watercolours were never meant to be in frames, rather they were stored flat in folios. Now we tend to mount and frame our watercolours, but it is imperative to use the right materials. Never use ordinary glue to mount the picture, as the glue will eventually seep through onto the picture, and always use acid-free board. If you are in any doubt at all, use a reputable professional framer.

Some 20 years ago it was the fashion to frame watercolours with wide mounts, often with lines drawn round where the mount meets the picture. Today there is more of a trend towards close-framing watercolours so that the mount is scarcely visible. It's up to your individual taste.

OCOLLECTING FRAMES

There is a thriving market in old frames today, with auction houses even dedicating sales purely to the sale of antique frames. In some cases the frames are more valuable than the pictures they encase. Intricate 17th- and 18th-century gilded and hand-carved frames are the most valuable, followed by handmade oak frames designed for Pre-Raphaelite pictures. Frame-making became more industrialized in Victorian times, with companies in the north of England reproducing hand-carved designs in cast plaster. These are not worth much today unless they are in perfect condition, which is rare.

Photographs and posters Large photographs and posters often look best behind a sheet of Perspex or plain glass. Fancy frames tend to detract from a photograph, especially black-and-white prints. Small photos, however, look better mounted, because we currently like photos to be A3-sized. If they are mounted, a simple thin black or gold frame looks best.
Protection Watercolours, photographs, and prints should always have a glass front, preferably non-reflective to prevent

the mirror effect. Paper can get dirty and damp easily, and you cannot dust a work on paper as you can oil or acrylic paintings, so this layer of glass will offer protection.

LIGHTING YOUR ARTWORKS

Technology has improved dramatically in the past few years, and there are now choices in the way you light artwork. The very worst way of illuminating a picture, for example, is a strip light fixed to the top of the frame. This used to be common practice, and countless pictures have been damaged because a strip light has been placed too near the canvas or watercolour. Ultraviolet rays bleach and fade the top of a piece, and infrared heat rays damage the paint, the canvas, and the frame. Heat damage is compounded when a light is turned off and on, as the picture suffers expansion and contraction each time the switch is flicked.

LIGHTING A PICTURE

There are three choices that apply to anything in a frame:
Picture lights If you want to use what is called a picture light (a tube bulb encased in brass or stainless steel with arms), make sure that the arms extend away from the picture. The distance between the picture and the light depends on the size of the picture, so visit a specialist lighting emporium with the measurements of your pictures. The expert there will calculate what size of light you need.
Ceiling lights A directional halogen light set in the ceiling will wash your picture with a warm glow and avoid hotspots (when one part of the picture is illuminated and another in shadow). Keep the halogen at a distance of about a quarter of the ceiling height. With larger pictures it might be a good idea to inset a halogen spotlight on either side of the picture.
Combination If you use a picture light suspended above a large picture (usually on a wall bracket) it is a good idea to add

a directional uplighter on a table; this will blur all the shadows that the picture light might create.

LIGHTING A SCULPTURE

The main concerns when lighting a sculpture or installation are to show off its three-dimensional quality, and to ensure that when admirers move around the piece they do not have a light shining directly into their face. It is best to employ two light sources in this case, both from above and directed. One halogen spotlight should be bright and the other half or a third as strong. The less powerful light goes some way towards softening the shadows without taking away from the drama of the sculpture.

LIGHTING TIP

Lights on a dimmer can offer a variety of moods. When you want a picture to stand out you can light it brightly, and when you want a quieter, more subtle atmosphere you can dim the lights.

CLEANING & RESTORING

When in doubt about whether to restore or clean a piece, then don't. Much physical damage has been done by using unsuitable chemicals in the name of restoration or cleaning. Often all that is needed is a dust with a soft cloth.

Sculpture Do not use polish or wax on stone or marble. Rather, apply a dry cloth softly; on very textured surfaces a new soft-bristled paintbrush can work well.

Oil paintings These should really be dusted with a feather duster; anything more abrasive might scratch the surface.

Prints and photographs You cannot really clean these items. Tiny insects can get under the glass, however, in which case open the frame and carefully remove them with a soft paintbrush.

IS A CLEAN PICTURE MORE VALUABLE THAN A DIRTY ONE?

A dirty Old Master is of greater interest to a dealer than one that has been cleaned. Pictures hauled from the dusty storeroom of an historic house appeal because they have not been seen by anyone else, and for this dealers put a premium on them. The same does not apply for a modern picture with flaking paint.

Recently, some auction houses have been pushing sellers to clean pictures in order to attract more interest from fellow members of the public, because most of us like clean pictures. However, by doing this you may be narrowing your options and putting off dealers. Conversely, as a buyer you will get a better deal on cleaned pictures. A non-trade buyer does not care whether the picture has been passed round the houses before. Also, as a private seller you will never recoup the cost of cleaning a picture

A well-established Old-Master restorer based in London, Patrick Corbett, knows a good way to sell a dirty picture. He points out that it is difficult to value a dust-encrusted painting that has been lying in an attic for years, and suggests that you put the idea to a trusted dealer that you sell him a 50% share, get him to get it cleaned and present it to clients. When he finds a buyer, split an agreed percentage of the profit. This is a good way of safeguarding the buyer's interest, because the value of this picture is unknown. In bad condition it may be worth very little, but expertly cleaned it could be worth ten times as much. The dealer gets to sell a hitherto unseen picture, which is good for their prestige.

RESTORATION

Restoration of artworks, most notably famous masterpieces such as Leonardo da Vinci's *Last Supper*, can be a highly controversial matter. The decision to restore an important piece is often taken when it is considered worth risking the integrity and the condition of a piece in order to preserve it for the future and reveal its original design and colour. As for your privately owned artworks, you should balance your desire to see them clean and complete with the risk of damaging them further. In any case, if you happen to be in possession of a grime-encrusted picture or one that is damaged, never attempt to restore it yourself: call in an expert. Equally, if you find a picture you love and the surface is not entirely smooth, do not worry, because any painting can be relined and restretched. The passage of time causes the wooden frame to which the canvas is attached to warp or collapse. Relining just means attaching a new back to the original canvas, which will prevent any more flaking and cracking of the paint caused by tension. However, ensure your restorer does not remove any old inscriptions or sale details that might have been on the back of the picture when transferring it to the new backing.

When a painting is stored in a cold, damp atmosphere a grey film known as a bloom can appear in the surface level of varnish. At first the picture is visible through this film, but if the picture is not brought into a drier and warmer environment and stored in the right place the bloom will turn yellow, possibly even black, making the painting unrecognizable. Expert restorers can remove this and many other kinds of dirty deposits that can build up on artworks.

USEFUL CONTACTS & REFERENCE

MOVING AND PACKING
See also pp.109 and 160–1 for the shipping and packaging firms EuroUSA, Art Move, Cadogan Tate, and Gander and White.
Fine Art Shipping Full service art handling and storage, local to Los Angeles and internationally. Visit www.fineartship.com or call +1 800 421 7464.
Northern Artery Fine art shipping, crating, installation, and storage for the United States, primarily serving the northeast corridor. Visit www.northernartery.com or call +1 207 283 0607 and toll free 877 283 0607.

RESTORATION AND CONSERVATION
Art Preservation Services New York-based APS specializes in preservation, with products relating to relative humidity and pollution. Visit www.apsnyc.com or call +1 212 722 6300.
British Association of Paintings Conservator-Restorers This

organization has well over 400 members in the UK and around the world. Find a conservator-restorer here. Visit www.bapcr.org.uk or call +44 (0)239 246 5115.

Conservator's emporium An American firm specializing in products for art conservation and restoration, including humidity control. Visit www.consemp.com or call +1 775 852 0404.

Deborah Bates This London studio conserves and restores all types of fine art on paper. Visit www.deborahbates.com or call +44 (0)20 7223 1629.

International Institute for Conservation of Historic and Artistic Works This organization can recommend a restorer. Visit www.iiconservation.org or call in the UK on +44 (0)20 7839 5975. Visit the American branch at http://aic.stanford.edu or call +1 202 452 9545.

J.S. Humidifiers plc This company supplies excellent machines to create the best atmosphere for pictures, as well as machines that monitor the level of humidity in a room. Visit www.jshumidifiers.com or call +44 (0)1903 850200.

FRAME COLLECTING

Arnold Wiggins and Sons Specialists in bespoke and antique frames, also with a repair and restoration service. Visit 4 Bury Street, London, SW1Y 6AB or call +44 (0)20 7925 0195.

Balfour & Wessels Framefinders Inc. This New York firm's stock ranges from 16th-century European pieces to American 20th-century Arts and Crafts examples. Visit www.framefinders.com or call +1 212 396 3896.

Eli Wilner & Company This New York art gallery specializes in American and European frames from the 19th to the early 20th century. Visit www.eliwilner.com or call +1 212 744 6521.

LIGHTING

John Cullen Lighting This London-based specialist lighting company will advise on lighting pictures. Visit www.johncullenlighting.co.uk or call +44 (0)20 7371 5400.

ART MOVEMENTS EXPLAINED

"Art evokes the mystery without which
the world would not exist."
René Magritte

What you will learn in this chapter:

- The difference between "Modern" and "Contemporary"
- The meaning of common terms used to describe art
  movements and styles

Nobody wants to show their ignorance – professionalism and
confidence are important when buying art, so it is good to
know your Abstract Expressionists from your Neo-Expressionists.
Generally artists themselves hate being given labels, but for
collectors it acts as a sort of shorthand when comparing and
contrasting artists. The artists listed in Movements, Schools,
& Styles, starting on p.174, include those who have had an
important influence on future generations or contemporaries in
each movement. By researching these artists – looking them up
on the Internet or in a library, or finding them in a museum –
you will find it easier to understand the different styles. If you
want to specialize in Conceptual art, for instance, then looking
at the best examples in museums will give you a base line from
which to assess less expensive practitioners.

The terms discussed in this chapter represent a selection
based on art movements that interest buyers today, and on

commonly confused terms. Firstly, one common confusion is that regarding the difference between the terms "modern" and "contemporary", so we will look at this first, before dealing with the multitude of labels that are used to categorize art styles and artists.

"CONTEMPORARY" VERSUS "MODERN"

Contemporary broadly means work by living artists, even if they are now very old. Christie's auctioneers reorganized their Contemporary Art Department in 2000, and now distinguish between international artists from the post-Second World War years to the end of the 1960s, which come under the Post War category, and Contemporary Art, which is strictly applied to work produced in the 1970s or later. Sotheby's, however, does not make such a distinction: their Contemporary Art department features works by artists who have been creating art since 1945. The Contemporary Art catalogues of Phillips de Pury in New York focus mainly on work from the 1980s onwards, though they do categorize Contemporary Art as being post-war onwards, and they have a separate "Impressionist and Modern Art" department. Bonhams' Modern and Contemporary Art Department encompasses the major art movements of the past 100 years, "ranging from blue-chip modern and post-war painting and sculpture to cutting-edge contemporary".

While "contemporary" has a relative, temporal meaning, "Modern Art", on the other hand, tends to be characterized by a rejection of old subjects. In particular, the term usually refers to art created from a period dating roughly from the 1860s to the 1970s. For example, by the end of the 19th century the church and religious foundations were no longer important patrons of the arts. Painters at the time, such as Courbet and Manet, rejected the historical and religious in favour of scenes from modern everyday life. Modern art emerged as part of the

West's attempt to acknowledge an industrial and secular society. The Impressionists went on to champion this break from tradition and the depiction of everyday subjects.

So there is clearly some overlap between these two terms, but as a general rule we can think of "Modern Art" as being art from Manet and the Impressionists up until the 1960s or 1970s, and "Contemporary Art" as art from the 1960s or 1970s up until this very minute – with some art fitting into both categories (or neither if it is a very a traditional, pedestrian piece from 1890, for example).

MOVEMENTS, SCHOOLS, & STYLES

Abstract Expressionism The best known Abstract Expressionists are American and worked directly after the Second World War – Jackson Pollock, Mark Rothko, Willem de Kooning, Barnett Newman, Robert Motherwell, and Philip Guston. They were influenced by the work of European artists fleeing Hitler, such as Max Ernst and Fernand Léger, as well as Kandinsky, Van Gogh, and the Surrealist Joan Miró. Abstract Expressionism was less a style than an attitude. For example, Mark Rothko and Jackson Pollock painted in very different manners, but were united in their pursuit of self-expression. Abstract Expressionists sought to capture an inner vision of reality – see "Expressionism" and "Colour Field Painting".

Arte Povera A recent exhibition in London reawakened interest in a group of Italy-based artists, who in the late 1960s produced sculpture, photography, and paintings. The name given to their group literally means "poor art", but this is misleading, because the artists were not poor and did not work with particularly poor materials. They sought to show that there was art in everyday objects, so they used everyday materials, and sometimes their work had a political slant. They had nothing in common stylistically, but showed together with the aim of challenging traditional media and subjects for art. Their techniques have since become extremely commonplace tools in Contemporary art. In fact this is one of the reasons why such a small and short-lived movement continues to have significance today. Some of the prime movers were Giovanno Anselmo, Alighiero Boetti, Luciano Fabro, Mario Merz, Pino Pascali, Giuseppe Penone, Emilio Prini, and Gilberto Zorio.

Barbizon School Before Claude Monet and Frédéric Bazille left Paris for Barbizon, a small village on the edge of the forest of Fointainebleau, in 1862 to work *en pleine air*, a group of artists had already been there, 30 years earlier. They, too emphasized the direct study of nature, and although totally eclipsed and not at all well known today, these members of the Barbizon School are worth looking at. The main Barbizon painters were Théodore Rousseau, Narcisse-Diaz de la Peña, Georges Michel, Jean-Baptiste-Camille Corot, and Charles-François Daubigny. Daubigny made an interesting collection of engravings and prints.

Colour Field Painting The Colour Field Movement of the 1960s followed on from the Abstract Expressionists, and was inspired by the works of Barnett Newman and Mark Rothko. Colour Field painters such as Canadian Jack Bush, Americans Ellsworth Kelly and Paul Jenkins, and German-Americans Helen Frankenthaler and Friedel Dzubas, among others, often painted an entire canvas in one or two colours to suggest that it was part of a larger field. Paint was applied in an even manner, and Colour Field Artists did not attempt to show feelings of depth or three-dimensionality. (*See* Hard-Edge Painting.)

Conceptual Art This is rather a broad term covering art that can be executed in a number of media – photographs, maps, videos, and more recently language (written and spoken). It can be said to be a more cerebral art form, concerning ideas rather than the art object for its own sake. Many of the world's best contemporary artists are Conceptual artists. Conceptual pieces are often created from ready-made materials, and Minimalist sculptors can be described as Conceptual artists. Arte Povera artists were often Conceptual artists too.

Author and expert Tony Godfrey explains in his book *Conceptual Art* (*see* Bibliography, p.188) that this form of artistic expression "is not about forms or materials but about ideas and meanings. It cannot be defined in terms of medium or style, but rather by the way it questions what art is. In particular Conceptual Art challenges the traditional status of the art object as unique, collectable, and saleable." Conceptual art is interactive and can require active participation. It asks the viewer to imagine something when they look at the work. Early conceptual artists were John Hilliard, Mel Bochner, Victor Burgin, Robert Barry, and Ana Mendieta. Other big names, who are very collectable today and command huge prices, are Joseph Beuys, John Baldesari, and Bruce Nauman.

Cubism This well-known movement began around 1907, led by Picasso and featuring Georges Braque, Fernand Léger, and Robert Delaunay. These artists broke with the tradition of a single viewpoint and attempted to represent the subject from multiple angles, fracturing the view, and later tending more and more to abstraction. To simplify, the aim of the initial "Analytic" phase was to show the object as the mind knows it to be rather than as the eye sees it. Works made during the second, "Synthetic", phase were composed of brighter, simpler forms.

Expressionism This term refers to art that tries to express emotions rather than an exact representation of nature. Some artists before the 20th century have elements of Expressionism in their work, but mostly this refers to artists in the early 20th century (c.1905–25), influenced by Vincent Van Gogh, Henri Matisse, Raol Dufy, André Derain, and Maurice de Vlaminck. These artists painted flowers and landscapes not as they actually look, but in bright colours to evoke an emotional response. Expressionism found particularly fertile ground in Germany, and the term German Expressionism is used to describe the work of Ernst Ludwig Kirchner, Erich Heckel, August Macke, and Gabriele Münter. Swiss-born Paul Klee and Russian Wassily

Kandinsky painted in the German Expressionist vibrant, colourful, and naïve manner. The Norwegian Edvard Munch's later work can also be linked to Expressionism.

Fauvism A short-lived (1905–8) movement – concurrent with and influencing Expressionism – of painting in vivid, exuberant, and non-naturalistic colours in order to express emotion via the sheer luminosity of the paint. As with Expressionism, it was heavily influenced by the work of Van Gogh. The name derives, as is often the case, from a critic's insult, which was happily adopted by the artists themselves: Louis Vauxcelles considered their art babaric – they were *fauves* (wild beasts). Key Fauvists include André Derain, Henri Matisse, Raoul Dufy, and Maurice de Vlaminck.

Futurism This was primarily an Italian art movement, which proclaimed its aims in an article in the French newspaper *Le Figaro* in 1909. Futurists wanted to modernize what they saw as the old-fashioned sculpture, painting, and architecture of the previous generations, focusing instead on speed and technology. The best-known Futurist painters are Umberto Boccioni, Luigi Russolo, and Carlo Dalmazzo Carrà, who were based in Milan. Christopher Nevinson is considered to be a British Futurist.

Hard-Edge Painting This is similar to Colour Field Painting, but instead of a smooth field of colour, geometric shapes in a limited palette are applied to the canvas in various patterns, which are often symmetrical. The term was coined in 1959 by art historian Jules Langsner to characterize the non-figurative work of several Californian artists, and it was cemented when British critic Lawrence Alloway used it to describe contemporary American geometric abstract painting featuring an "economy of form", "fullness of colour", and "neatness of surface". Hard-edge painters include Kenneth Noland, who painted chevron-patterned compositions, Karl Benjamin, Frederick Hammersley, Lorser Feitelson, and John McLaughlin.

Hudson River School This first school of American painting was founded by the artist Thomas Cole in the 1820s and was centred round New York. The artists of the school, who painted in oil and watercolour, also included Asher B. Durand, Albert Bierstadt, Frederic Edwin Church, Jasper Francis Cropsey, George Caitlin, George Inness, Thomas Moran, and Francis A. Silva. They believed it was the painter's role to depict the ideal landscape on a beautiful day as God had made it. Landscapes were for the moral edification of citizens, who were to be amazed at the Lord's work.

Impressionism The famous late-19th-century French art movement in which artists such as Claude Monet, Alfred Sisley, Camille Pissarro, Edgar Degas, and Pierre Auguste Renoir worked in the open air in order to capture the essence of everyday scenes under their specific atmospheric conditions, using pure light colours in small dabs that combined to create a fleeting "impression". (*See* Post-Impressionism and Neo-Impressionism.)

Minimalism This is the negation of self-expression. Although artists such as Malevich had founded Minimalist art at the beginning of the 20th century by placing a black square on a white ground, Minimalism really became popular in 1950s America as a backlash against "slushy" Abstract Expressionism. Minimalists work in any medium – such as oil on canvas or ready-made materials such as wood, glass, or steel. They do not carve out of stone, and there are no soft lines in their work. Minimalism is one of the art movements people find hard to understand because of the lack of craftsmanship in the work. For example, people may ask: "How can a Formica cupboard be art?" However, its simplicity can have wide appeal, and museum shows of Minimalist art do well. Carl Andre, Dan Flavin, Donald Judd, Sol Le Witt, and Robert Morris are famous Minimalists, and they are very blue chip.

Neo-Expressionism Neo-Expressionists turned their backs on the introspective nature of Expressionism. Working during the 1970s and 1980s, they abandoned restraint and adopted traditional methods again: smaller paintings on easels and carved sculpture. Their imagery incorporated everything from classical mythology to the covers of trashy novels. It is an international movement and no one can recall who first used this term, which encompasses a huge variety of work. Major artists of the movement include the Americans Julian Schnabel, David Salle, and Jean-Michel Basquiat, the Italians Sandro Chia and Francesco Clemente, Chema Cobo and José Maria Sicilia from Spain, Anselm Kiefer and Rainer Fetting from Germany, Per Kirkeby from Denmark, and Christopher Le Brun from Britain.

Neo-Impressionism After Impressionism there was a generation of Post-Impressionists, some of whom called themselves Neo-Impressionists. Neo-Impressionists were much more rule-bound, in part due to the development in the science and understanding of colour, and believed that it was possible to replicate nature on a canvas by following certain techniques and rules – although different rules applied to each artist. There was no formula to suit all. Techniques associated with Neo-Impressionists are Pointillism, where dots of paint make up the whole, and Divisionism, which involves the separation of colour through separate brushstrokes of pigment. Georges Seurat, Paul Signac, and Camille Pissarro were prime movers in this movement. Divisionism was more popular in Italy, where it was practised by Angelo Morbelli, Vittore Grubicy, and Giovanni Segantini. (*See* Post-Impressionism.)

Norwich School The beautiful light depicted by painters who worked around Norwich, England in the early part of the 19th century is timeless, and so the famous names of the Norwich School will always be valuable. Prime movers in the Norwich School were John Crome, John Sell Cotman, and James Sillett and they had many followers. Cotman had two sons who painted – Miles Edmund, who used both oils and watercolour, and John Joseph, who painted mainly in oil and gave his pictures strong atmospheres. It could be said that the broad washes of J.S. Cotman's watercolours anticipate Impressionism.

Op Art This is short for Optical Art – as in optical illusion – and came to the public notice in an exhibition at the Museum of Modern Art in New York entitled *The Responsive Eye* in 1965. Op Art is always abstract and often creates the illusion of movement. Bridget Riley from Britain is the most famous exponent, and given the recent rise in price for her work it would be wise to watch and see if others working in this field start to escalate in price too. Other Op artists include Yaacov Agam (Israeli); Richard Anuszkiewicz, Larry Poons, and Larry Zox (American); and Victor Vasarely (Hungarian-French).

Pop Art This term stands for Popular Art, which was a reaction against the more cerebral Abstract Expressionism. Pop artists' imagery was taken from everyday life, whether advertising hoardings or American icons: Jasper Johns' depictions of the American flag, Roy Lichtenstein's homage to comic books, and Warhol's screen prints of Marilyn Monroe are famous Pop Art images. By taking aspects of popular culture and consumerism and turning them into art, these artists could be mocking the art establishment, providing a critique of materialism, or simply using images that were most relevant to them and the age in which they lived.

The movement is thought to have started in England when Richard Hamilton showed his photomontage *Just What Is It That Makes Today's Homes So Different, So Appealing?* in 1956. American Pop artists John Dine, Johns, Lichtenstein, and Warhol have become very valuable and blue chip, but British Pop artists Richard Hamilton, Peter Blake, Joe Tilson, and Ron Kitaj have failed to reach the prices of their American counterparts. Today British art collectors buy either more traditional forms of art or international modern art. American collectors of Pop Art, meanwhile, do not rate British artists as highly as their own.

Post-Impressionism The eighth and last Impressionist exhibition was held in Paris in 1886 and the term Post-Impressionist was coined by Roger Fry in 1910 for an exhibition in London at the Grafton Gallery. We all know the Impressionists, but remember that Paul Cézanne, Paul Gauguin, Vincent Van Gogh, and Georges Seurat are Post-Impressionists, although many began as Impressionists. They rejected the Impressionists' concern for atmosphere and light in favour of stronger, more colourful, more expressionistic images. Post-Impressionist art had an enormous influence on later generations of artists. (See Neo-Impressionism.)

Postmodernism "Postmodern" is a term bandied about liberally, and as a result its parameters are ill-defined. Author and art critic Daniel Bell used the phrase in his book *The End of Ideology*, which was published in 1960 (see Bibliography, p.188). The term is more easily comprehensible in reference to architecture. A postmodern architect adds flourishes to a building – such as a pediment or a window detail – in reaction to the style of Mies van de Rohe and the Bauhaus architects, whose ideal was pure structure free from embellishments. Postmodernism is less used in reference to painters and sculptors, but can sometimes refer to artists who have eschewed abstract and Minimalist work in favour of the figurative.

Surrealism This is central to the development of Modern art, and the Belgian René Magritte and the Spaniard Salvador Dalí are household names. Surrealism is another loosely used term, but in relation to art it refers to work that, in the words of André Breton, is pure psychic automatism – "thought dictated in the absence of control exerted by reason, and outside all aesthetic or moral preoccupations". There is often no rhyme or reason to the subject matter of Surrealist paintings, which may seem weird and fantastic, or portray physically impossible scenarios.

Surrealism was primarily a European movement, and other big names include Jean Arp (German), André Masson and Yves Tanguy (French), Meret Oppenheim (Swiss), and Dora Carrington and Grace Pailthorpe (British). The Surrealists had a considerable influence in Latin America, for exmaple on the writings of Buenos Aires-born author Jorge Luis Borges.

Symbolism At the end of the 19th century the Symbolist painters in France sought to portray a world that was not invaded by machines and the Industrial Revolution. They were motivated by the spiritual, and in some cases the occult, and their work has a dream-like quality, including subjects from myth and allegory as well as contemporary life. Puvis de Chavannes, Odilon Redon, Gustave Moreau, Henri Fantin Latour, and Aristide Maillol are the most representative names from this movement. The Norwegian Edvard Munch worked as a Symbolist in the 1890s, before graduating to more Expressionist works.

Vorticism Vorticism was a British-based art and literary movement founded in 1914 by Wyndham Lewis, editor of the magazine *Blast: Review of the Great English Vortex,* which owed its name to Ezra Pound. The aim was to blast away all Victorian fussiness in favour of modern energy. Pound asserted that the centre of this energy was the vortex, and that the artist's work focuses round a strong central core. Vorticists placed machines, a symbol of the modern age, at the centre of their work. They included the painters Edward Wadsworth, William Roberts, and Wyndham Lewis, the sculptors Jacob Epstein and Henri Gaudier-Brzeska, and the photographer Alvin Langdon Coburn. The Vorticists' work has never commanded the prices of more international art movements, such as Expressionism and Abstract Expressionism, but a recent London exhibition of Wyndham Lewis' work may help to attract more public attention to this area of art.

DIRECTORY

Please also refer to individual chapters for relevant contacts. While every effort has been made to ensure entries are up-to-date, readers are advised to confirm details by telephone before making any long trips. Remember that the principal auction houses – Sotheby's, Christie's, and Bonhams – have salerooms or representatives throughout the UK and the rest of the world, so if you want to find one near you, use the contact details given under their London headquarters entries below.

AUCTION HOUSES

UNITED KINGDOM

LONDON

Bloomsbury Auctions Ltd
Bloomsbury House,
24 Maddox Street W1S 1PP
Tel: +44 (0)20 7495 9494
www.bloomsburyauctions.com

Bonhams
101 New Bond Street W1S 1SR
Tel: +44 (0)20 7629 6602
www.bonhams.com

Christie's
8 King Street, St James's
SW1Y 6QT
Tel: +44 (0)20 7839 9060
www.christies.com

Sotheby's
34–5 New Bond Street
W1A 2AA
Tel: +44 (0)20 7293 5000
www.sothebys.com

REGIONAL

Anderson & Garland
Anderson House, Crispin Court,
Newbiggin Lane, Westerhope,
Newcastle upon Tyne NE5 1BF
Tel: +44 (0)191 430 3000
www.andersonandgarland.com

Bearnes
St Edmund's Court,
Okehampton Street,
Exeter EX4 1DU

Tel: +44 (0)1392 207000
www.bearnes.co.uk

Bourne End Auction Rooms
Station Approach, Bourne End,
Buckinghamshire SL8 5QH
Tel: +44 (0)1628 531500

Brightwells Fine Art
The Fine Art Saleroom,
Easters Court, Leominster,
Herefordshire HR6 0DE
Tel: +44 (0)1568 611122
www.brightwells.com

Canterbury Auction Galleries
40 Station Road West,
Canterbury, Kent CT2 8AN
Tel: +44 (0)1227 763337
www.thecanterburyauction
galleries.com

Capes Dunn & Co
The Auction Galleries,
38 Charles Street, off Princess
Street, Gr. Manchester M1 7DB
Tel: +44 (0)161 273 6060

Cato Crane & Co
Liverpool Auction Rooms,
6 Stanhope Street,
Liverpool L8 5RF
Tel: +44 (0)151 709 5559
www.cato-crane.co.uk

Charterhouse
The Long Street Salerooms,
Sherborne, Dorset DT9 3BS
Tel: +44 (0)1935 812277
www.charterhouse-
auctions.co.uk

Cheffins
Clifton House, Clifton Road,
Cambridge CB1 7EA
Tel: +44 (0)1223 213343
www.cheffins.co.uk

David Lay (ASVA)
Action House, Alverton,
Penzance, Cornwall TR18 4RE
Tel: +44 (0)1736 361414

Dee, Atkinson & Harrison
The Exchange Saleroom,
Driffield, Yorkshire YO25 6LD
Tel: +44 (0)1377 253151
www.dahauctions.com

Dreweatt Neate
Donnington Priory,
Donnington, Newbury,
Berkshire RG14 2JE (and others)
Tel: +44 (0)1635 553553
www.dnfa.com

Gorringes Auction Galleries
Terminus Road, Bexhill-on-Sea,
East Sussex TN39 3LR
Tel: +44 (0)1424 212994
www.gorringes.co.uk

John Ross & Company
37 Montgomery Street,
Belfast, Co. Antrim,
Northern Ireland BT1 4NX
Tel: +44 (0)28 9032 5448

Keys
Off Palmers Lane, Aylsham,
Norfolk NR11 6JA
Tel: +44 (0)1263 733195
www.aylshamsalerooms.co.uk

DIRECTORY

Lyon & Turnbull
33 Broughton Place,
Edinburgh EH1 3RR
Tel: +44 (0)131 557 8844
www.lyonandturnbull.com

Morphets of Harrogate
6 Albert Street,
Harrogate HG1 1JL
Tel: +44 (0)1423 530030
www.morphets.co.uk

Neales
192 Mansfield Road,
Nottingham NG1 3HU
Tel: +44 (0)115 962 4141
www.neales-auctions.com

Rupert Toovey & Co Ltd
Spring Gardens, Washington,
West Sussex RH20 3BS
Tel: +44 (0)1903 891955
www.rupert-toovey.com

**Thomson, Roddick
& Medcalf Ltd**
Coleridge House,
Shaddongate,
Carlisle CA2 5TU
(and others)
Tel: +44 (0)1228 528939
www.thomsonroddick.com

Wingett's Auction Gallery
29 Holt Street, Wrexham,
Clwyd, Wales LL13 8DH
Tel: +44 (0)1978 353553
www.wingetts.co.uk

Wintertons Ltd
Lichfield Auction Centre,
Fradley Park, Lichfield,
Staffordshire WS13 8NF
Tel: +44 (0)1543 263256
www.wintertons.co.uk

Woolley & Wallis
Salisbury Salerooms,
51–61 Castle Street,
Salisbury, Wiltshire SP1 3SU
Tel: +44 (0)1722 424500
www.woolleyandwallis.co.uk

AUSTRALIA
Leonard Joel Auctioneers
333 Malvern Road,
South Yarra, Victoria 3141
Tel: +61 (0)3 9826 4333
www.ljoel.com.au

Shapiro Auctioneers
162 Queen Street, Woollahra,
Sydney NSW 2025
Tel: +61 (0)2 9326 1588

AUSTRIA
Dorotheum
Palais Dorotheum, A-1010
Wien, Dorotheergasse 17,
1010 Vienna
Tel: +43 515 60 229
www.dorotheum.at

BELGIUM
Bernaerts
Verlatstraat 18-22, 2000
Antwerpen/Anvers
Tel: +32 (0)3 248 19 21
www.auction-bernaerts.com

CANADA
Ritchies Inc.
288 King Street East,
Toronto, Ontario M5A 1K4
Tel: +1 416 364 1864
www.ritchies.com

Waddington's Auctions
111 Bathurst Street,
Toronto M5V 2R1
Tel: +1 416 504 9100
www.waddingtonsauctions.com

MEXICO
Galeria Louis C. Morton
GLC A7073L IYS, Monte Athos
179, Col. Lomas de
Chapultepec CP11000
Tel: +52 5520 5005
www.lmorton.com

REPUBLIC OF IRELAND
Hamilton Osborne King
4 Main Street,
Blackrock, Co. Dublin
Tel: +353 1 288 5011
www.hok.ie

James Adam & Sons
26 St Stephen's Green,
Dublin 2
Tel: +353 1 6760261
www.jamesadam.ie

Thomas P Adams & Co
38 Main Street,
Blackrock, Co Dublin
Tel: +353 1 288 5146

Whyte's Auctioneers
38 Molesworth Street,
Dublin 2
Tel: +353 1 676 2888
www.whytes.ie

SWEDEN
Bukowski's
Arsenalsgatan 4, Stockholm
Tel: +46 8 614 08 00
www.bukowskis.se

SWITZERLAND
Galerie Koller
Hardturmstrasse 102,
8031 Zürich
Tel: +41 (1) 445 63 31
www.galeriekoller.ch

UNITED STATES
**The Coeur d'Alene Art
Auction**
PO Box 310, Hayden ID 83835
Tel: +1 208 772 9009
www.cdaartauction.com

Rachel Davis Fine Arts
1301 West 79th Street,
Cleveland OH 44102
Tel: +1 216 939 1191
www.racheldavisfinearts.com

Doyle New York
175 East 87th Street,
New York NY 10128
Tel: +1 212 427 2730
www.doylenewyork.com

Jackson's Auctioneers & Appraisers
2229 Lincoln Street,
Cedar Falls IA 50613
Tel: +1 319 277 2256

James D Julia, Inc.
PO Box 830, Rte. 201
Skowhegan Road,
Fairfield ME 04937
Tel: +1 207 453 7125
www.juliaauctions.com

Kimball M Sterling, Inc.
125 West Market Street,
Johnson City,
Tennessee 37601
Tel: +1 423 928 1471
www.outsiderartauctions.com

Leslie Hindman, Inc.
122 North Aberdeen Street,
Chicago, Illinois 60607
Tel: +1 312 280 1212
www.lesliehindman.com

New Orleans Auction Galleries, Inc.
801 Magazine Street,
AT 510 Julia, New Orleans,
Louisiana 70130
Tel: +1 504 566 1849

Phillips, de Pury & Co.
450 West 15 Street,
New York NY 10011
Tel: +1 212 940 1200
www.phillipsdepury.com

Shannon's
354 Woodmont Road,
Milford, Connecticut 06460
Tel: +1 203 877 1711
www.shannons.com

Skinner Inc.
63 Park Plaza, Boston MA 02116

Tel: +1 617 350 5400
www.skinnerinc.com

Sloan's & Kenyon
4605 Bradley Boulevard,
Bethesda, Maryland 20815
Tel: +1 301 634 2330
www.sloansandkenyon.com

Treadway Gallery, Inc.
2029 Madison Road,
Cincinnati, Ohio 45208
Tel: +1 513 321 6742
www.treadwaygallery.com

MUSEUMS

UNITED KINGDOM

Aberdeen Art Gallery
Schoolhill, Aberdeen AB10 1FQ
Tel: +44 (0)1224 523700
www.aagm.co.uk

Ashmolean Museum
Beaumont St, Oxford OX1 2PH
Tel: +44 (0)1865 278000
www.ashmol.ox.ac.uk

Barbican Art Gallery
Silk Street, London EC2
Tel: +44 (0)20 7638 4141
www.barbican.org.uk

British Museum
Great Russell Street,
London WC1B 3DC
Tel: +44 (0)20 7323 8299
www.thebritishmuseum.ac.uk

Courtauld Institute
Somerset House, Strand,
London WC2R 0RN
Tel: +44 (0)20 7848 2777
www.courtauld.ac.uk

Hayward Gallery
Royal Festival Hall, Belvedere
Road, London SE1 8XX
Tel: +44 (0)20 7921 0813
www.hayward.org.uk

Leeds City Art Gallery
The Headrow, Leeds LS1 3AA

Tel: +44 (0)113 247 8248
www.leeds.gov.uk/artgallery

Manchester Art Gallery
Mosley Street,
Manchester M2 3JL
Tel: +44 (0)161 235 8888
www.manchestergalleries.org

National Gallery
Trafalgar Square,
London WC2N 5DN
Tel: +44 (0)20 7747 2885
www.nationalgallery.org.uk

National Galleries of Scotland (Various)
Tel: +44 (0)131 624 6200
www.natgalscot.ac.uk

National Portrait Gallery
St Martin's Place,
London WC2H 0HE
Tel: +44 (0)20 7306 0055
www.npg.org.uk

National Museum of Wales
Cathay's Park, Cardiff CF10 3NP
Tel: +44 (0)29 2039 7951
www.nmgw.ac.uk

Royal Academy of Arts
Burlington House,
Piccadilly, London W1J 0BD
Tel: +44 (0)20 7300 8000
www.royalacademy.org.uk

Saatchi Gallery,
County Hall, Southbank
London SE1 7PB
Tel: +44 (0)20 7928 8195
www.saatchi-gallery.co.uk

Tate Britain
Millbank, London SW1P 4RG
Tel: +44 (0)20 7887 8000
www.tate.org.uk

Tate Liverpool (website above)
Albert Dock, Liverpool L3 4BB
Tel: +44 (0)151 702 7400

Tate Modern (website above)
Bankside, London SE1 9TG
Tel: +44 (0)20 7887 8000

DIRECTORY

Tate St Ives (website p185)
Porthmeor Beach, St Ives,
Cornwall TR26 1TG
Tel: +44 (0)1736 796226
Ulster Museum
Botanic Gardens,
Belfast BT9 5AB
Tel: +44 (0)28 9038 3000
www.ulstermuseum.org.uk
Whitechapel Art Gallery
80–2 Whitechapel High Street,
London E1 7GX
Tel: +44 (0)20 7522 7888
www.whitechapel.org

AUSTRALIA
**Art Gallery of
New South Wales**
Art Gallery Road, The Domain,
Sydney NSW 2000
Tel: +61 2 9225 1700
www.artgallery.nsw.gov.au
National Gallery of Australia
Parkes Place,
Canberra ACT 2601
Tel: +61 2 6240 6502
www.nga.gov.au

AUSTRIA
Academy of Fine Arts Vienna
A-1010 Vienna, Schillerplatz 3
Tel: +43 (0)1588 16 (ext.135)
www.akbild.ac.at

BELGIUM
Palais des Beaux-Arts
23 rue Ravenstein,
B-1000 Brussels
Tel: +32 2 507 84 44

CANADA
**Montreal Museum
of Fine Arts**
PO Box 3000, Station H,
Montreal, Quebec H3G 2T9

Tel: +1 514 285 1600
www.mmfa.qc.ca
National Gallery of Canada
380 Sussex Drive, Box 427,
Station A, Ottawa,
Ontario K1N 9N4
Tel: +1 613 990 1985
national.gallery.ca

FRANCE
**Centre National d'Art et de
Culture Georges Pompidou**
Place Georges Pompidou,
75004 Paris
Tel: +33 (0)1 44 78 12 33
www.cnac-gp.fr
The Louvre
36 Quai du Louvre, 75058 Paris
Tel: +33 (0)1 40 20 50 50
www.louvre.fr
Musée d'Orsay
63 rue de Lille, 75343 Paris
Tel: +33 (0)1 40 49 48 14
www.musee-orsay.fr

GERMANY
Deutsche Guggenheim Berlin
Unter den Linden 13-15,
10117, Berlin
Tel: +49 (0) 30 20 20 93 0
www.deutsche-guggenheim-
berlin.de
Hamburger Kunsthalle
Stifung öffenlichen Rechts,
Glockengießerwall,
20095 Hamburg
Tel: +49 40 428 131 200
www.hamburger-kunsthalle.de

HOLLAND
Rijksmuseum
Stadhouderskade 42,
1071 20 Amsterdam
Tel: +31 (0)20 6747000
www.rijksmuseum.nl

ITALY
**National Gallery
of Modern Art**
Viale delle Belle Arti 131,
00196 Rome
Tel: +39 (0)6 322 98 1
www.gnam.arti.beniculturali.it
Uffizi Gallery
Piazzale degli Uffizi,
50122 Firenze
Tel: +39 (0)55 2388 651
www.polomuseale.firenze.it

JAPAN
Nat. Museum of Modern Art
3 Kitanomaru Koen,
Chiyoda-ku, Tokyo 102-8322
Tel: +81 03 5777 8600
www.momat.go.jp
Nat. Museum of Western Art
7-7 Ueno-Koen, Taito-ku,
Tokyo 110-0007
Tel: +81 03 3828 5131
www.nmwa.go.jp

NEW ZEALAND
Auckland Art Gallery,
Corner Wellesley & Kitchener
Streets, Auckland
Tel: +64 9 307 7700
www.aucklandartgallery.govt.nz
Christchurch Art Gallery
Worcester Boulevard/Montreal
Street corner, Christchurch
Tel: +64 3 941 7300
www.christchurchartgallery.
org.nz

RUSSIA
**Pushkin State Museum
of Fine Arts**
121019 Moscow,
12 Volkhonka Street
Tel: +7 203 79 98
www.museum.ru/gmii

State Hermitage Museum
34 Dvortsovaya Naberezhnaya
(Palace Embankment),
St Petersburg 190000
Tel: +7 812 710 96 25
www.hermitagemuseum.org

SPAIN
Guggenheim Museum Bilbao
Abandoibarra Et. 2,
48001 Bilbao
Tel: +34 94 435 90 80
www.guggenheim-bilbao.es
Museo del Prado
P del Prado s/n, 28014 Madrid
Tel: +34 91 330 28 00
museoprado.mcu.es

UNITED STATES
The Art Institute of Chicago
111 South Michigan Avenue,
Chicago, Illinois 60603
Tel: +1 312 443 3600
www.artic.edu
Solomon R. Guggenheim Museum, 1071 Fifth Avenue
at 89th Street, New York
Tel: +1 212 423 3500
www.guggenheim.org
Institute of Contemporary Art (ICA)
955 Boylston Street,
Boston MA 02115
Tel: +1 617 266 5152
www.icaboston.org
Metropolitan Museum of Art
1000 Fifth Avenue at 82nd St,
New York, NY 10028-0198
Tel: +1 212 535 7710
www.metmuseum.org
National Portrait Gallery
Smithsonian Institution,
8th and F Streets, NW

Washington, DC 20560
Tel: +1 202 275 1738
www.npg.si.edu

GALLERIES

Here is a small selection of commercial galleries. See *also* the Useful Contacts & Reference in chapter three and on p.110.

UNITED KINGDOM
LONDON
Advanced Graphics London
32 Long Lane SE1 4AY
Tel: +44 (0)20 7407 2055
www.advancedgraphics.co.uk
Art First
First Floor,
9 Cork Street W1S 3LL
Tel: +44 (0)20 7734 0386
www.artfirst.co.uk
The Coningsby Gallery
30 Tottenham Street W1
Tel: +44 (0)20 7636 7478
www.coningsbygallery.com
The Hospital
24 Endell Street WC2H 9HQ
Tel: +44 (0)20 7170 9100
www.thehospital.co.uk
Victoria Miro Gallery
16 Wharf Road N1 7RW
Tel: +44 (0)20 7336 8109
www.victoria-miro.com

REGIONAL
Albany Gallery
74b Albany Rd,
Cardiff CF24 3RS
Tel: +44 (0)29 2048 7158
www.albanygallery.com
The Biscuit Factory
16 Stoddart Street, Newcastle
upon Tyne NE2 1AN

Tel: +44 (0)191 261 1103
www.thebiscuitfactory.com
Firstsite
The Minories Art Gallery,
74 High Street, Colchester,
Essex CO1 1UE
Tel: +44 (0)1206 577067
www.firstsite.uk.net
Ingleby Gallery
6 Carlton Terrace,
Edinburgh EH7 5DD
Tel: +44 (0)131 556 4441
www.inglebygallery.com
North House Gallery
The Walls, Manningtree
Essex CO11 1AS
+44 (0)1206 392717
www.northhousegallery.co.uk

UNITED STATES
Roy Boyd Gallery
739 N. Wells Street,
Chicago IL 60610
Tel: +1 312 642 1606
www.royboydgallery.com
James Cohan Gallery
533 West 26th Street,
New York, NY 10001
Tel: +1 212 714 9500
Jane Haslem Gallery
2025 Hillyer Place NW,
Washington, DC 20009
Tel: +1 202 232 4644
www.janehaslemgallery.com
Pace Wildenstein
32 E.57th Street,
New York, NY 10022
Tel: +1 212 421 3292
www.pacewildenstein.com
Tracy Williams Ltd
313 West 4th Street
New York, NY 10014
Tel: +1 212 229 2757
www.tracywilliamsltd.com

BIBLIOGRAPHY

Please see also "Useful Contacts & Reference" at the end of each chapter.

Ackerman, Marcus S. *Smart Money and Art: Investing in Fine Art* (Station Hill Press, Barrytown, NY, 1986)

Atkins, Robert *ArtSpeak: A Guide to Contemporary Ideas, Movements and Buzzwords, 1945 to the Present* (Abbeville Press, New York, 1990)

Barnicoat, John *Concise History of Posters* (Thames and Hudson, World of Art series, London, 1972)

Batchelor, David *Minimalism* (Tate Publishing, Movements in Modern Art series, London, 1997)

Bell, Daniel *The End of Ideology* (Harvard University Press, Cambridge, MA, 1965)

Crofton, Ian (Editor) *Dictionary of Art Quotations* (Routledge, London, 1988)

Godfrey, Tony *Conceptual Art* (Phaidon, *Art & Ideas* series, London, 1998)

Goldman, Paul *Looking at Prints, Drawings and Watercolours: A Guide to Technical Terms* (British Museum Press, London, 1988)

Lewis, B. et al. *Minimalism* (catalogue) (Tate Gallery Liverpool, 1990)

Mallalieu, Huon *How to Buy Pictures* (Christies' Collectors Guides, Phaidon, London, 1984)

Mallalieu, Huon *Understanding Watercolours* (Antique Collectors' Club, Woodbridge, 1985)

Martin, Judy *Longman Dictionary of Art: A Handbook of Terms, Techniques, Materials, Equipment and Processes* (Longman, Harlow, 1986)

Nadeau, Luis *Encyclopedia of Printing, Photographic, and Photomechanical Processes, A–Z*, Vols. 1 & 2 (Atelier Luis Nadeau, New Brunswick, 1989–90)

Paul, Christiane *Digital Art* (Thames and Hudson, World of Art series, London, 2003)

Rosenthal, Norman *Sensation: Young British Artists from the Saatchi Collection* (Thames and Hudson, London, 1998)

Snoddy, Theo *Dictionary of Irish Artists: 20th Century* (Wolfhound Press, Dublin, 1996)

Stanley-Baker, Joan *Japanese Art* (Thames and Hudson, London, 1984/2000)

Tregear, Mary *Chinese Art* (Thames and Hudson, London, 1997)

Turner, Jane (Editor) *The Grove Dictionary of Art* (Macmillan and Co., Basingstoke, 1996; and others)

Walsh, John (Editor) *Bill Viola: The Passions* (J. Paul Getty Museum, LA, 2003)

Wilmerding, John *Signs of the Artist: Signatures and Self Expression in American Painting* (Yale University Press, New Haven, CT, 2004)

PERIODICALS

To really know what's happening, where to buy, and learn some art history, it is worth buying or subscribing to one of the magazines listed below. Some may cover your specific interests more than others. Nowadays museum shops and good bookshops sell titles devoted to art. (*See also* p.21).

Art & Antiques Magazine A monthly American magazine. It always covers a painting issue along with a broad sweep of subjects, such as collecting posters. Tel: +1 815 734 1162, www.artandantiques.net. Published by Trans World Publishing Inc., Atlanta.

Art in America Provides a good mix of what's going on, old and new, from around the world. Articles are more in-depth than in *Art & Antiques*. Tel: +1 212 941 2806, www.artinamericamagazine.com. Published by Brant Art Publications, New York.

Art Monthly UK journal with a leaning towards contemporary art. Tel: +44 (0)20 7240 0389, www.artmonthly.co.uk. London.

ARTNews American topic-based magazine, for instance with articles about new collectors, Nazi war loot, auction news. Tel: +1 212 398 1690, www.artnewsonline.com. Published by Circulation Specialists Inc., South Norwalk, CT.

The Art Newspaper International news diary in tabloid format, which might cover big donors, government policy towards the arts, or what Charles Saatchi is buying. Tel: +44 (0)20 7735 3331 (UK) or +1 212 343 0727 (US), www.theartnewspaper.com. Published by Umberto Allemandi e C., Torino.

Art Review Glossy London-based monthly magazine that also covers stories from the United States and Europe. Art meets fashion and interior design. Tel: +44 (0)20 7236 4880 (UK) or +1 212 727 3400 (US), www.art-review.com. Published by Art Review Ltd., London.

The British Art Journal Learned journal publishing original research on British art with long, detailed essays on a wide variety of issues. www.britishartjournal.co.uk. Enquiries to Sally Sharp, Holborn Direct Mail, Rothsay House 2–6 Rothsay St, London SE1 4UD, fax +44 (0)20 7357 6065.

Galleries Magazine available free at galleries, with previews and news listings arranged by areas of London and the UK, and a list of galleries and artists whose work you can view online. Tel: +44 (0)20 8740 7020, www.artefact.co.uk. Published by Barrington Publications, London.

Modern Painters A quarterly magazine with, for example, excellent in-depth studies of Russian art or short analyses of pictures. Literary meets arty; top notch contributors are often well-known authors or artists. Tel: +44 (0)20 7407 9247, www.modernpainters.co.uk. Published by Fine Arts Journals Ltd.

INDEX

INDEX

ACKNOWLEDGMENTS

Thanks to: Patrick Corbett, picture restorer; Pierre Valentin of Withers lawyers; Sarah Hamilton
without whom this book would be still be a pile of papers; and Claire Musters and Catherine
Emslie, my editors.

QUOTE SOURCES

p.8: *The Shock of the New*, Robert Hughes, Thames & Hudson, London, 1991; p.14: "Art
& Money", *The New Art Examiner*, Robert Hughes,1984, from a Harold Rosenberg Memorial
Lecture; p.22: anon; p.34: the play *Pity in History*, Howard Barker, 1985; p.98: "Discourse VI",
Seven Discourses on Art, Joshua Reynolds, 1774, delivered to RA students on distribution of prizes;
p.112: André Breton – *Dictionary of Art Quotations* (*see* p.188); p.130: Leonardo Da Vinci –
www.artquotes.net; p.142: Rome Jorge, *The Manila Times*, 10th April 2004; p.150: Jonathan
Jones, *The Guardian*, September 4, 2003; p.162: Jackson Pollock – www.artquotes.net;
p.165: James Rosenquist – www.artquotes.net; p.172: René Magritte – www.artquotes.net